Kaṭha Upaniṣad

Rediscovering Indian Literary Classics

(ISSN - 0972-0111)

1. Taittirīya Upaniṣad: With the Original Text in Sanskrit and Roman Transliteration; by Muni Narayana Prasad. (ISBN 978-81-246-0014-6)

2,4-5. Bṛhadāraṇyaka Upaniṣad: With Original Text in Roman Transliteration. English Translation and Appendices; by Nitya Chaitanya Yati; Vol. 1: Madhu Kāṇḍa; Vol. 2: Muni Kāṇḍa; Vol. 3: Khila Kāṇḍa. (ISBN 978-81-246-0008-5)

3. Kena Upaniṣad: With the Original Text in Sanskrit and Roman Transliteration; by Muni Narayana Prasad. (ISBN 978-81-246-0034-4)

6. Muṇḍaka Upaniṣad: With the Original Text in Sanskrit and Roman Transliteration; by Muni Narayana Prasad. (ISBN 978-81-246-0105-1)

8. Praśna Upaniṣad: With the Original Text in Sanskrit and Roman transliteration; by Muni Narayana Prasad. (ISBN 978-81-246-0129-7)

9. Aitareya Upaniṣad: With the Original Text in Sanskrit and Roman transliteration; by Muni Narayana Prasad. (ISBN 978-81-246-0142-6)

10. Śrī Dakṣiṇāmūrti Stotram of Śrī Śaṅkarācārya; with the commentary Tattva Prakāśikā; by Tattvavidananda Saraswati; Edited by Puppala B. (ISBN 978-81-246-0210-2)

11. Āditya Hṛdayam: With the Commentary Tattvaprakāśikā; by Tattvavidananda Saraswati (ISBN 978-81-246-0231-7)

12. Vāstuśāstra: Ancient Indian Architecture and Civil Engineering — Retrospects and Prospects; by Rahul Kumar Altekar (ISBN 978-81-246-0246-1)

13. Gaṇapati Upaniṣad: With the Commentary Tattvaprakāśikā; by Tattvavidananda Saraswati (ISBN 978-81-246-0265-2)

14. Life's Pilgrimage Through the Gītā; by Muni Narayana Prasad (ISBN 978-81-246-0310-9)

15. Chāndogya Upaniṣad: With the Original Text in Sanskrit and Roman transliteration; by Muni Narayana Prasad (ISBN 978-81-246-0374-1)

16. Īśāvāsya and Māṇḍūkya Upaniṣads: With the origiinal text in Sanskrit and Roman Transliteration by Muni Narayana Prasad (ISBN: 978-81-246-0492-2)

Rediscovering Indian Literary Classics, no. 7

Kaṭha Upaniṣad

with the original text in
Sanskrit and Roman transliteration

Translation with
an Extensive Commentary
by
Swami Muni Narayana Prasad

PRINTWORLD
Publishers of Indian Traditions

Cataloging in Publication Data — DK
[Courtesy: D.K. Agencies (P) Ltd. <docinfo@dkagencies.co.

Narayana Prasad, *Muni*, 1938-
Kaṭha Upaniṣad.
(Rediscovering Indian literary classics; no. 7)
ISBN 13: 9788124601105

1. Upanishads. Kaṭhopaniṣad — Commentaries.
2. Hinduism — Sacred books. I. Upanishads.
Kaṭhopaniṣad. English & Sanskrit. II. Title.
III. Series: Rediscovering Indian literary classics; no. 7.

ISBN 13: 978-81-246-0110-5
First published in India in 1998
Second impression in 2004
Third impression in 2014

Published and printed by:
D.K. Printworld (P) Ltd.
Regd. office : *Vedaśrī*, F-395, Sudarshan Park
(Metro Station: Ramesh Nagar)
New Delhi - 110 015
Phones : (011) 2545-3975; 2546-6019; *Fax* : (011) 2546-5926
e-mail: indology@dkprintworld.com
Web: www.dkprintworld.com

Preface

WHEN I joined the *Gurukula* as a teenager, reciting the texts of the Upaniṣads, short ones in full and select portions of the long ones, was what I found most interesting in the daily routine of life there. I was taught the way of proper recitation by Nitya Chaitanya Yati, then one of the senior disciples of Nataraja Guru, and now the Guru and Head of the Narayana Gurukula. And in some cases, Nataraja Guru directed us on how to introduce alterations that would better the traditional orthodox way of recitation. Years later I also began to teach the Gurukula children this recitation as well as the meaning of these Upaniṣads in as simple a way as possible. The texts thus recited and taught were compiled into a book we named the *Gurukula-Dhyāna-Mañjuṣā*. Upon my finally deciding to take *sannyāsa,* Nataraja Guru gave me these words of direction:

Every sannyasin has his own pattern of *sannyāsa*. You need not imitate me. As one who has been holding firm to the Upaniṣads from the very beginning, you may better adopt a life based on the firm ground of the Upaniṣads and their teachings. At that moment I resolved to dedicate myself to delving into the subtleties of the philosophical vision contained in the words of the Upaniṣads. In time I realised that the best way of doing this was to write down what I was able to see there. The *Kaṭha Upaniṣad* was the first of these. The outcome was initially serialized in the Malayalam philosophical monthly *The Gurukulam* and later in the *Gurukulam Quarterly* published from the Narayana Gurukula Centre in the United States. Both were well received by readers and this inspired me to take up the other Upaniṣads as well. Years later upon re-reading what I had written on the *Kaṭha Upaniṣad*, I felt that it lacked clarity, a natural defect of immature thought. So I rewrote the entire commentary, putting it into the shape you now see it in.

In the *Gurukula,* formal recitation of Upaniṣads accompanies the *homa* (symbolic fire-sacrifice) held on Sundays and special occasions such as the annual Gurukula convention. Nataraja Guru, in the discourse that customarily followed the *homa*, would elucidate on the text, giving important hints on the dialectical way of searching for the hidden wisdom of the *Upaniṣad*. These hints have constantly been guiding me in the writing of this commentary. Many vital points have also been highlighted, by a group of research scholars getting together and pondering over each of these verses. The present commentary, is thus the result of a collective effort.

In the meantime Guru Nitya Chaitanya Yati and I also took up the grand project of putting together the Narayana Gurukula's commentaries to all the ten major Upaniṣads: He was to write on the *Bṛhadāraṇyaka* and *Chāndogya* and I, on the rest. Guru had already written a commentary to *Māṇḍūkya*. In effect I had to handle the remaining seven. My commentaries on the *Īśa Upaniṣad* have already appeared in a different format in the *Basic Lessons on India's Wisdom*. The *Bṛhadāraṇyaka* commentary of Guru Nitya is already available in print in three volumes. The present book is part of this project. Towards the materialisation of this project, Messers D.K. Printworld of New Delhi have started a new series entitled 'Rediscovering Indian Literary Classics'. Guru Nityas' Commentary on the *Chāndogya* is in the making.

Kala Ramesh of Bangalore, a long-time associate of the Gurukula Movement, found time to edit the book carefully in spite of all her other responsibilities. She did it out of her sheer love for wisdom. A *sannyāsin* is indebted to none and having no social obligation; I do not dare to express my indebtedness to her.

If I have at any point deviated from the familiar traditional way, it is less out of disrespect, and more out of a desire to state as clearly as I could what I found in these Upaniṣads. I was all the time guided by the great Masters, my own Guru and the light of modern scientific thought. What is substantiated basically is the *Advaita* philosophy of Śaṅkara as revalued and restated by Sri Narayana Guru.

With due homage to the long line of Gurus, beginning with Ādi Nārāyaṇa, I offer this mind-flower at the feet of Guru Nitya Chaitanya Yati.

Varkala
10.4.1998 **Swami Muni Narayana Prasad**

Contents

Introduction

ALL Upaniṣads teach *brahmavidyā*, the Science of the Absolute, whose ultimate goal is to free the seeker from the tangle of worldly trials and tribulations of day-to-day life. This freedom is known as *mukti* or *mokṣa*.

The Upaniṣads appear as appendices to the four Vedas: *Ṛg*, *Yajur*, *Sāma* and *Atharva*. The Vedas are the primordial expression of knowledge of the Aryan culture and the most ancient of all recorded material. The *Yajurveda* has two declensions: *Śukla* (the white) and *Kṛṣṇa* (the black), and the *Kaṭha Upanisad* forms part of the latter.

Vedānta is the name popularly used for the wisdom of the Upaniṣads, though, literally meaning 'the end of knowledge', *veda* meaning knowledge, and *anta*, end. It is so called because the Upaniṣads constitute the terminal part of the Vedas, and philosophically, it is the wisdom beyond which nothing remains to be known.

The Vedas concern themselves mainly with rituals called *yajñas*, such as burnt sacrifices. Though *yajñas* were highly symbolic of pure wisdom to start with, in the long run they degenerated into exercises in priestcraft, and those who performed them became completely oblivious of the real import. To salvage the submerging beacon of wisdom from the corrupted current of Vedic ritualism, the *Katha Upanisad* made its dramatic apprearance.

This Upaniṣad unravels the mystery of death, and in the course of it, expounds the whole of *brahmavidyā*. Death and life are both a mystery; one meaningless without the other. But man, in his ignorance is entranced with life and abhors death the inevitable. He is terrified of advancing old-age and the approach of death, and remains disturbed like Shakespear's Hamlet who says, "death, the undiscovered country, from whose bourn no traveller returns, puzzles the will". Science too stands puzzled before this inevitable phenomenon of life. No one knows exactly what death is, what happens at death and what, if anything, continues to exist after death, and how. It is around this enigma that the teaching of the *Kaṭha Upaniṣad* revolves. The God of death himself teaches Naciketaṣ, the secret of death — the immortality of the Real.

The setting of this Upaniṣad is the aftermath of one of the most famous *yajña*s — the Viśvajit meaning, the conqueror of the universe. At the close of such rituals, it is enjoined in the Vedas that the sacrificer should gift all his worldly belongings to the priests. Vājaśravas, the man who here has conducted the Viśvajit, is shown giving priests a *dakṣiṇa* of cows too old to eat and drink, too old to bear young or yield milk, symbolic of how far Vedic ritualism had degenerated. Giving away useless cows as gift has the double benefit of relieving the giver of the burden of having to maintain them, and effortlessly fulfilling a religious injunction. Such possiblities for exploiting situations do exist in ritualism. The seeker of Truth, uncorrupted by worldly interest and avarice, saves himself and others from such viciousness. To see the truth as it is needs an uncorrupt and unprejudiced mind, and Naciketas, the young seeker in this Upaniṣad, the son of Vājaśravas, is one such. Little children, as Jesus taught, possess an innocence which deserves the Kingdom of Heaven. The *Kaṭha Upaniṣad,* both historically and philosophically, thus occupies a unique position in Indian thought.

शान्तिपाठः

ओं सह नाववतु। सह नौ भुनक्तु। सह वीर्यं करवावहै।
तेजस्वि नावधीतमस्तु। मा विद्विषावहै।।

ॐ शान्तिः। शान्तिः। शान्तिः।

oṁ saha nāv avatu । *saha nau bhunaktu* ।
saha vīryaṁ karavāvahai । *tejasvi nāv adhītam astu* ।
mā vidviṣāvahai ॥
oṁ śāntiḥ । *śāntiḥ* । *śāntiḥ* ॥

May (God) protect us both. May He save us both. (May both of us enjoy together). May we attain vigour together. Let what we learn be illumined. May we not be hostile to each other.

Auṁ Peace! Peace! Peace!

Wisdom teaching takes place between master and disciple — a dialectical situation where the two are counterparts, between whom wisdom becomes illumined. The need for rapproachment between a true master (*sad-guru*) and a true disciple (*sat-śiṣya*) in the wisdom-teaching context has been sufficiently made clear in the Chapter 'Guru and Śiṣya' of the book *The Word of the Guru* by Nataraja Guru. The establishment of this bipolarity is a rare occurrence, as a favourable chance element it has a major role to play. The present Peace Invocation is a prayer of the master and the disciple together for strengthening the bond between them, so that an effective and fruitful illumination of wisdom may occur. The finality of wisdom is attained only by those who seek it for its own sake, and are satisfied with nothing less than the ultimate Truth. Though one is an enthusiastic seeker, one need not necessarily gain wisdom if living under unfavourable circumstances. Many, in spite of favourable conditions, fail to gain wisdom as their desire and resoluteness are not strong enough. Sometimes true seekers, though blessed with favourable circumstances and a strong mind, are deterred, finding no true guide. Chance, or the grace of God alone, brings all these elements together. The prayer here asks for this grace. Secret wisdom (the meaning of the word *upaniṣad*), remains a secret, of no value to others and to posterity, unless imparted by a master to a true seeker. No master true to the word Guru, which means dispeller of darkness, can keep his wisdom concealed; he necessarily has to expose himself — his self — to the one who seeks. Wisdom is thus illumined, and both the master and the disciple become self-satisfied, the former in having played his true role and the latter in experiencing the fulfilment of life. Both together therefore pray for such an illumination and fulfilment.

The love and compassion of the master towards the disciple and the disciple's trust in the Guru and his words are the main cementing elements in their mutual adoption. A disciple suspicious of the veracity of the Guru's teaching, in effect, doubts Truth itself, and as the *Bhagavad Gītā* reminds, 'The suspicious one perishes' (IV.40). Whole-hearted trust in the Truth and the Guru and an earnest and dedicated attempt on the part of the seeker enable him to attain the goal. The prayer here is thus also for both master and disciple to be saved from mutual distrust and hatred.

Wisdom is sought for nothing other than the peace it brings. According to Indian Philosophy, three kinds of suffering are appeased on gaining Wisdom: self-caused sufferings (*ādhyātmika duḥkha*), those caused by others (*ādhibhautika duḥkha*) and the ones caused by God or the natural course of events (*ādhidaivika duḥkha*). The three invokings to bestow peace indicate the desire for the appeasement of all three kinds of suffering.

Part I

Chapter I

प्रथमा वल्ली

ॐ उशन् ह वै वाजश्रवसः सर्ववेदसं ददौ ।
तस्य ह नचिकेता नाम पुत्र आस ।। १ ।।

oṁ uśan ha vai vājaśravasaḥ sarvavedasaṁ dadau ।
tasya ha naciketā nāma putra āsa ।। 1 ।।

Desirous of the fruits (of the Viśvajit sacrifice) the son of Vājaśravā, as the story goes, gave away all his wealth (after the sacrifice). He had a son, Naciketas by name.

THE *Kaṭha Upaniṣad*, in order to draw a contrast between the values represented by Vedic ritualism and Vedāntic Wisdom, is set in the context of a *yajña*. Sacrifices are performed with earthly and heavenly pleasures for benefits, and depend on the correctness and efficacy with which the ritual is performed as well as the blessing of the gods. Ritual is thus of relative value. Wisdom, depending upon nothing but oneself, one's self-knowledge, is of absolute value, both endwise and meanswise. A sacrificer (*yajamāna*), as the Vedic injunctions have it, should give away, at the end of the Vivśajit, all his wealth to priests. Even these injunctions are followed with an element of deception by the present sacrificer, just to convince others, showing how far ritualism could degenerate. The wisdom teaching that follows, relying on self-awareness alone, does not succumb to such fraudulence. The Upaniṣad beginning in the form of a parable, according to Śaṅkara, is meant to glorify *vidyā* (wisdom) as against *avidyā* (ignorance).

Even the name Vājaśravā is suggestive; the word means one whose fame (*śravaḥ*) owes itself to the giving away of food (*vāja*) as a pious act. Vājaśravā was a man who became famous for public feeding, a *pūrta karma.** Vājaśravā being of the habit of spending only a part of his savings for public benefit, his son Vājaśravasaḥ, though desirous of performing one of the important *yajñas*, need not be expected to spend all his wealth on it, though it be a part of the Vedic injunction concerning the Viśvajit. What was important for him, was becoming a conqueror of the world (as the name of the *yajña* itself indicates) rather than being true to the spirit of the sacrifice and the tradition. This shows his lack of knowledge. Dishonesty accompanies ignorance and appears in the sacrificial situation, and eventually clears the path for pure wisdom, with Naciketas as its torch-bearer.

तं ह कुमारं सन्तं दक्षिणासु नीयमानासु श्रद्धाऽऽविवेश; सोऽमन्यत ॥ २ ॥

taṁ ha kumāraṁ santaṁ dakṣiṇāsu nīyamānāsu śraddhā"viveśa; so'manyata ॥ 2 ॥

Faith (*śraddhā*) took possession of the good youngster as the gifts were being taken away by the priests. He thought:

Naciketas notices the deceptive way in which his father gave away religious gifts, and is filled with the yearning for honesty (*śraddhā*). Only such innocent minds can revamp corrupt ritualism and bring in pure wisdom.

He observes his father performing his religious duty, and finding him lacking honesty, he feels the urge to correct his father. However Indians traditionally consider that children ought not to correct their parents, a custom which originally prompted parents to keep themselves their children's ideals, so that they had no chance to find fault with them. Caught between the urge to correct his father and the child's obligation, he thinks:

*In India, religious acts are classified as *iṣṭa karma*, which include burnt sacrifices, leading an austere life, maintaining truthfulness, protecting the Vedic tradition, etc., and *purta karma*, which includes such acts as digging public wells and pools, planting shade trees, constructing camp-sheds for travellers, public feeding, and the like.

पीतोदका जग्धतृणा दुग्धदोहा निरिन्द्रियाः ।
अनन्दा नाम ते लोकास्तान् स गच्छति ता ददत् ।। ३ ।।

pītodakā jagdhatṛṇā dugdhadohā nirindriyāḥ ।
anandā nāma te lokās tān sa gacchati tā dadat ।। 3 ।।

Joyless are the worlds one goes to on giving away as gifts cows that have stopped drinking water, eating food and yielding milk and lost vitality.

To have a joyful life here and to attain a joyful life hereafter are my father's aims in performing this ritual. Now, on its completion, he is distributing cows as gifts to the priests; but they are dry and barren, too old to eat and drink. The very scriptures which my father followed in performing this ritual warn against such gifts: those who give such gifts go to joyless worlds, the opposite of what my father intends attaining. Such gifts, of no use to the receiver, are offered simply to get rid of the burden of keeping them. Avarice-ridden, he does not think of his having to receive benefits which are the exact opposite to what he aimed at. Worldly pleasures were his interest when perfoming this ritual. He is not honest even to it. How far away he would be then from knowing the utlimate Reality that ensures eternal Happiness! He has to be corrected; but how can I, his son, do it? However, I must try; not directly, but by asking him to offer me, the most precious of all his wealth.

स होवाच पितरं तत कस्मै मां दास्यसीति ।
द्वितीयं तृतीयं तं होवाच मृत्यवे त्वा ददामीति ।। ४ ।।

sa hovāca pitaraṁ tata kasmai māṁ dāsyasīti ।
dvitīyaṁ tṛtīyaṁ taṁ hovāca mṛtyave tvā dadāmīti ।। 4 ।।

He asked his father, "O Father, to whom are you going to offer me?" He asked him a second time, a third time. Then the father said, "To Death I offer you."

"Dear father, I am your son. A son is everything to his father, so giving away one's son means giving away everything. You may thus fulfil your obligation to give away everything you possess."

Naciketas, thus, while being dutiful and obedient as a son, indirectly reminds his father of his obligation, and equally indirectly tries to save him from the ill-effects of his dishonesty.

Unmindful of Naciketas's purity of mind and honesty, the father, with a mind blirred too much by worldly interests, did not answer at first. A father instinctively tries to keep his son always with him. The boy, insistent, asked the same question a second time, and a third time, causing the father irritation. Without stopping to think what he was saying, the father replies, "To Death I offer you".

These angry words of his father, set Naciketas, the loving son that he was, to thinking:

बहूनामेमि प्रथमो बहूनामेमि मध्यमः ।
किं स्विद् यमस्य कर्तव्यं यन्मयाद्य करिष्यति ।। ५ ।।

bahunām emi prathamo bahūnām emi madhyamaḥ ।
kiṁ svid yamasya kartavyaṁ yan mayādya karişyati ।। 5 ।।

Among many I am superior (as a son); among many I am (at least) the middling (as a son). What could be the obligatory duty my father intends to fulfil by offering me to Yama?

Unexpected as the reaction of the father was, Naciketas, on hearing it, broods over it. He, among many sons in this world, if not of a superior order, is at least of the middle order, in no case of the lowest. A superior (*uttama*) son is the one who strictly follows his father's instructions true to its spirit; a middling (*madhyama*) son is the one who follows his father's words true to the letter; the lowest (*adhama*), one who does not care for his father at all.

Naciketas's conscience feels that his father's words should not go in vain. Yet he ponders over, what his father would gain, what religious duty he would be fulfilling, by giving him away to Yama, the God of Death.

Though this action of his father is going to be beneficial to Naciketas, in bringing him learning of the secret of life and death from Death himself, his father, whose intent is only the gaining of worldly benefit, would get nothing by offering him to Death who is propitiated by none for favours. The only favour at his disposal is death! These reflections of Naciketas are indicative of the impossiblity of gaining wisdom unless one is willing to go beyond the world of pleasures, and become interested in the ultimate problem of life and death. Yet, the duties of a son, which are worldly values, are not neglected by him. Only those who are able to perceive all life values, worldly as well as spiritual, as different hierarchical grades in which one Reality finds self-expression, realize the real meaning of life and death. For them, worldly values are also a means to attain higher wisdom.

अनुपश्य यथा पूर्वे प्रतिपश्य तथापरे ।
सस्यमिव मर्त्यः पच्यते सस्यमिवाजायते पुनः ।। ६ ।।

anupaśya yathā pūrve pratipaśya tathā'pare ।
sasyam iva martyaḥ pacyate sasyam ivājāyate
punaḥ ।। 6 ।।

Father, look back and see what happened to your ancestors; look around and see what happens to others. Man decays and dies like corn; man emerges again like corn.

Naciketas's father, possibly regretting his inadvertently cruel words, is being consoled by the son who is not worried, though destined to go to Death to fulfil his father's words. It would appear that he was anticipating the meeting with Death, in order to learn from him the secret of death, whereas the father was worried about the impending loss of his son. A contrast between two value-worlds is here represented by the son and the father.

Man, apparently, is born, grows up and withers like vegetables, but what is distinctive of human life is the value-notions man inherits from his ancestors, and those he fashions out of his own day-to-day life. Such values, eternal in nature, which marks the loftiness of human nature, transcends the transitory nature of worldly life. Fully aware of such values, Naciketas does not want his father's words to go unheeded.

The scene is thus being set for unravelling the most fundamental of all problems — that of death — with Naciketas, questioning Death, playing the role of the earnest seeker (known as *pūrva-pakṣa* — the inciting questioner in the Vedāntic parlance). Only one endowed with this inborn value discrimination, like Naciketas, is competent to play this role.

वैश्वानरः प्रविशत्यतिथिर्ब्राह्मणो गृहान् ।
तस्यैतां शान्तिं कुर्वन्ति हर वैवस्वतोदकम् ॥ ७ ॥

vaiśvānaraḥ praviśaty atithir brāhmaṇo gṛhān ।
tasyaitāṁ śāntiṁ kurvanti hara vaivasvatodakam ॥ 7 ॥

A brāhmaṇa guest entering a house is like fire; hosts, to put the fire down, make pacifying offerings. O Death, please bring water for him.

On being given permission by the father, after being consoled by his son, Naciketas reached the abode of Death, but had to wait there, starving, three days and three nights. The text does not make it clear whether it was owing to the absence of Yama in the palace or because he wanted to test the earnestness of the new seeker. The *ṛṣi* of the Upaniṣad studiedly leaves it vague, enabling the reader to construe both meaning, the former of worldly significance related to hospitality and the latter a spiritual one, a test of the earnestness of the student. The scene is so set that the former leads to the latter.

To be received and honoured as a guest was not the intention of Naciketas, but his being so treated helps establish his competence as a student of *brahmavidyā*. The prerequisite qualities of a true wisdom-seeker, indicated in the Upaniṣads in a scattered fashion, have been codified by Śaṅkara: They are, the capability to discriminate between eternal and transient values (*nitya-anitya viveka*), a sense of detachment towards transient values (*vairāgya*), self-cultivation of six characteristics, namely, *śama* (checking and turning away the mind from distractions), *dama* (self-restraint by withdrawing the sense-organs from objects), *uparati* (non-dependence on the external), *titikṣā* (endurance), *śraddhā* (full faith in the words of one's Guru and of the scriptures) and *samādhāna* (to have thoughts of *Brahman* always in mind) and finally aspiration for final liberation (*mumukṣutva*).

Naciketas proves himself endowed with all such qualities.

Not having been informed of Naciketas's intention yet, Yama's attendants, considering him a guest of honour, requisition Yama to bring water, flowers and other things and receive him formally. Custom in India has it that a brāhmaṇa guest entering a house is like fire, to be appeased immediately by pouring water on his feet, offering flowers and then offering a seat and of course a sweet drink. Having had to starve three days increases the fieriness in Naciketas in the attendants' perception, making them a little nervous, and so they appear to be in a hurry. This makes way for Naciketas and Yama to establish the contact, which begins as a worldly one, but eventually is transformed into a spiritual one.

आशाप्रतीक्षे संङ्गतं सूनृतां च
इेष्टापूर्ते पुत्रपशूंश्च सर्वान् ।
एतद् वृङ्क्ते पुरुषस्याल्पमेधसो
यस्यानश्नन् वसति ब्राह्मणो गृहे ।। ८ ।।

āśā-pratīkṣe saṅgataṁ sūnṛtāṁ ca
iṣṭā-pūrte putra-paśūṁś ca sarvān ।
etad vṛṅkte puruṣasya alpa medhaso
yasyānaśnan vasati brāhmaṇo gṛhe ।। 8 ।।

Hopes and aspirations, results of intimacy with the noble and hearing their words, sacrifices and charities, sons and cattle and all else are taken away from the person in whose house a brāhmaṇa had to remain unfed.

A guest in the house, as the ancient Indian notion of hospitality goes, is to be treated as a visiting god. To feed a guest, the host is willing to go hungry. The *Taittirīya Upaniṣad* teaches:

mātṛ devo bhava, pitṛ devo bhava ।
ācārya devo bhava, atithi devo bhava ।।

Be one to whom mother is like a god;
Be one to whom father is like a god;
Be one to who one's teacher is like a god:
Be one to whom a guest is like a god.

(I.6)

A starving guest, in effect, portents loss of fame of the family, loss of all the property, loss of all acquired merits. This worldly notion is made instrumental here to prepare the ground for a wisdom teaching situation: The error of not honouring the visiting guest is repaired by Yama's offering Naciketas three boons, one for each day that he starved.

तिस्रो रात्रीर्यदवात्सीर्गृहे मे
अनश्नन् ब्रह्मन्नतिथिर्नमस्यः ।
नमस्तेऽस्तु ब्रह्मन् स्वस्ति मेऽस्तु
तस्मात् प्रति त्रीन् वरान् वृणीष्व ।। ९ ।।

tisro rātrīr yad avātsīr gr̥he me
anaśnan brahmann atithir namasyaḥ ।
namaste'stu brahman svasti me'stu
tasmāt prati trīn varān vr̥ṇīṣva ।। 9 ।।

I make obeisance to you, O brāhmaṇa, a guest of honour, who had to stay three nights in my residence unfed. May well-being be unto me. To make amends for the wrong, please choose three boons.

Giving Naciketas the opportunity to freely ask three boons, in the guise of mending a wrong done to him, Yama here gets a good chance to test how prone to worldly desires is Naciketas. It is on such occasions that deep-lying desires are stirred up to come to surface. Having already seen how resolute Naciketas is, it remains to be seen, as the second stage of Yama's testing, what are the things he is interested in.

शान्तसङ्कल्पः सुमना यथा स्याद्-
वीतमन्युर्गौतमो माभि मृत्यो।
त्वत्प्रसृष्टं माभिवदेत् प्रतीत
एतत् त्रयाणां प्रथमं वरं वृणे ।। १० ।।

śānta-saṁkalpaḥ sumanā yathā syād-
vītamanyur gautamo mābhi mr̥tyo ।
tvat prasr̥ṣṭaṁ mābhivadet pratīta
etat trayāṇāṁ prathamaṁ varaṁ vr̥ṇe ।। 10 ।।

Let Gautama (my father) — with allayed anxiety, anger gone, gracious towards me, recognizing me — greet me and speak to me with joy when set free by you. This I choose as the first of the three boons.

Anxious about his father, Naciketas, on hearing Yama's offer, chooses as his first boon, that his father be in a gracious mood, not angry with him anymore.

Final liberation, the goal of all Upaniṣadic teaching, can be attained only by those who are vigorous enough to free themselves of the ever binding tentacles of worldly relationships, not despicable in themselves, but because they are hurdles on the way to the goal.

After receiving the teaching of the secret of death from Death himself, and becoming *vimr̥tyuḥ* (the deathless one) — as shown in the concluding verse of the Upaniṣad — Naciketas's father, living still in fear of death, may not recognize him; so he prays to Yama that his father may recognize and receive him, as any father would, on getting back a lost son. On recognizing him, knowing him as deathless, the father would also possibly become desirous of getting the wisdom that makes one deathless.

That the teaching of the Upaniṣad in general, is not against upholding worldly values insofar as they are not hindrance to higher wisdom, is also implicit in Naciketas choosing this first boon.

यथा पुरस्ताद् भविता प्रतीत
औद्दालकिरारुणिर्मत्प्रसृष्टः ।
सुखं रात्रीः शयिता वीतमन्यु-
स्त्वां ददृशिवान् मृत्युमुखात् प्रमुक्तम् ।। ११ ।।

yathā purastād bhavitā pratīta
auddālakir āruṇir mat-prasr̥ṣṭaḥ ।
sukhaṁ rātrīḥ śayitā vīta-manyus-
tvāṁ dadr̥śivān mr̥tyu-mukhāt pramuktam ।। 11 ।।

As he had been before, Auddālaki Āruṇi, your father, seeing you released from the jaws of death, his anger gone, through my favour will sleep happily many a night.

Yama the god of death grants the first boon. In the next two verses Naciketas chooses the second boon.

स्वर्गे लोके न भयं किञ्चनास्ति
न तत्र त्वं न जरया बिभेति ।
उभे तीर्त्वाशनायापिपासे
शोकातिगो मोदते स्वर्गलोके ।। १२ ।।

svarge loke no bhayaṁ kiñcanāsti
na tatra tvaṁ na jarayā bibheti ।
ubhe tīrtvāśanāyāpipāse ।
śokātigo modate svargaloke ।। 12 ।।

No fear prevails in the heavenly world. You (death) too do not exist there; nor is there the fear of old-age. Having crossed over both hunger and thirst, leaving sorrow behind, one rejoices in that world.

स त्वमग्निं स्वर्ग्यमध्येषि मृत्यो
प्रब्रूहि तं श्रद्दधानाय मह्यम्।
स्वर्गलोकाः अमृतत्वं भजन्ते
एतद् द्वितीयेन वृणे वरेण ।। १३ ।।

sa tvam agniṁ svargyam adhyeṣi mṛtyo
prabrūhi taṁ śraddadhānāya mahyam ।
svarga-lokāḥ amṛtatvam bhajante
etad dvitīyena vṛṇe vareṇa ।। 13 ।।

O Death, such as you are, you know the fire (sacrifice) that leads one to heaven. Please teach me that (fire sacrifice) owing to which the dwellers of heaven gain immortality. This I choose as my second boon.

It was the happiness of his family, a happiness of the world here and now, that Naciketas ensured through the first boon. Through the second one he prays for the happiness of heaven, the conceptual world that the Vedas with their fire sacrifices aspire to attain.

Evidently Naciketas relinquishes neither of the worlds; instead he gives them the value they deserve and then goes beyond to the realm of

Supreme Happiness, aimed at by Vedāntic wisdom, which he is about to choose as the third boon.

The immortality (*amr̥tatva*) that characterises the dwellers of heaven mentioned here, is different from the Immortality, also known as *amr̥tatva*, which comes from the attainment of wisdom. The immortality of heavenly beings is conceived with the mortality of earthly beings as its negative side, while the Vedāntic Immortality is that of the non-dual Reality that unfolds itself as both the heaven of immortal beings and the earth of mortal beings. The superiority of heaven is relative to the inferiority of earth, and thus the Vedic concept of the immortality of heavenly beings is a relative one. Vedāntic Immortality, not of any particular being but of the one Reality, is absolute.

प्र ते ब्रवीमि तदु मे निबोध
स्वर्ग्यमग्निं नचिकेतः प्रजानन् ।
अनन्तलोकाप्तिमथो प्रतिष्ठां
विद्धि त्वमेतं निहितं गुहायाम् ।। १४ ।।

pra te bravīmi tad u me nibodha
svargyam agniṁ naciketaḥ prajānan ।
ananta-lokāptim atho pratiṣṭhāṁ
viddhi tvam etaṁ nihitaṁ guhāyām ।। 14 ।।

(Yama said:) Knowing well as I do, that heaven-reaching fire, I shall instruct you on it. Learn it from me. Know it, the means of attaining the boundless world, its support too, as abiding in the secret abode (of understanding).

लोकादिमग्निं तमुवाच तस्मै
या इष्टका यावतीर्वा यथा वा ।
स चापि तत् प्रत्यवदद् यथोक्त-
मथास्य मृत्युः पुनरेवाह तुष्टः ।। १५ ।।

lokādim agniṁ tam uvāca tasmai
yā iṣṭakā yāvatīr vā yathā vā ।
sa cāpi tat pratyavadad yathoktam
athāsya mr̥tyuḥ punar evāha tuṣṭaḥ ।। 15 ।।

Death taught him the fire sacrifice, existing since the world's beginning, (as also) what kind of bricks, how many, in what manner, are to be arranged for building the sacrificial pit. He (Naciketas), on his part, repeated the whole just as he was taught. Death, thus pleased with him, said again:

Vedic culture, of which Vedānta is an outgrowth, has for its pivot fire sacrifice. Vedāntic teaching therefore mostly assumes the garb of revision and revaluation of certain Vedic concepts, giving them a new dimension and a new meaning which is more profound, the present Upaniṣad perhaps the best instance of it.

Ritual and the joys of heaven are not what is intended to be taught in the Upanisad, and therefore the details of the fire sacrifice taught by Yama are deliberately left out.

The fire-principle or the principle of fire sacrifice, termed here *lokādi* implies that it marks the origination of the world and has been in existence since the beiginning of the world. It may be seen as the heat principle that operated in the emergence of the world. Thales, in the West, was the first philosopher who conceived of fire as the one basic principle behind multiple worldly appearances. In the Vedas and the Upanisads too there are references to a primordial person (*puruṣa*) undergoing *tapas*, a self-heating process, in order to bring forth the world out of himself. A heating takes place in our consciousness also as we delve deep into the subtler aspects of reality. Even our physical existence relies on self-created warmth. Life on earth depends on the heat and energy absorbed from the Sun. The fire-principle, in short, is so basic that without it there would be no life. Man who turns his attention to basic truths necessarily realizes this, and feels obliged to pay homage to fire, and use fire as the carrier of all human wishes to the gods. Thus emerged the *yajña* or fire-sacrifice, a concept that has found place in all religions and all cultures, in one or another way.

When put into practice as a religious rite enjoined in the Vedas, the formal aspects of this principle became more pronounced at the cost of the underlying meaning, making of it a binding religious duty. Its performing has to be true to the letter, failing which the intended results would not accrue. The way of ritual is rigid, unlike the way of wisdom which is not obligatory, depending only on self-knowledge. The contrast is made clear by Yama's instruction to Naciketas as to what kind of bricks are to be laid, how to lay them and so on. Naciketas, by the same token, gets fully familiar with the ritualistic aspect of Vedism, which the *Muṇḍaka Upaniṣad* called *aparā-vidyā*, and Kant, knowledge of the immanent. Ground is thus prepared for crossing over to the side of the *parā-vidyā*, the transcendental knowledge, the essence of the Upaniṣad.

Rāmānuja would easily find in these passages of the Upaniṣad clear support for his dear doctrine that Vedāntic wisdom is always to be preceded by full familiarity with Vedism and its ritual.

तमब्रवीत् प्रीयमाणो महात्मा
वरं तवेहाद्य ददामि भूयः ।
तवैव नाम्ना भवितायमग्निः
सृङ्कां चेमामनेकरूपां गृहाण ।। १६ ।।

tam abravīt prīyamāṇo mahātmā
varaṁ tavehādya dadāmi bhūyaḥ ।
tavaiva nāmnā bhavitāyam agniḥ
sṛṅkāṁ cemām aneka-rūpāṁ gṛhāṇa ।। 16 ।।

Delighted extremely, the high-minded (Yama) told him: I give you now one more boon: by your name shall this (sacrificial) fire be known. Also take this necklace of multiple beauty as a gift.

Yama, extremely pleased with Naciketas proving his worth as a student, grants him one more boon: "By your name shall hereafter be known this heaven-leading sacrificial fire." In the Vedic tradition this particular sacrificial fire is still known as *Nāciketāgni*. This incident indicates also how fully Naciketas imbibed the spirit and practical aspects of the sacrifice he was taught.

Yama, in addition, offers him a necklace of gems — probably the one he himself was wearing — of multiple beauty. The gem, most coveted of all worldly wealth, symbolizes heavenly pleasures Naciketas has made his own through imbibing the spirit of the fire sacrifice. The Vedic instruction of Yama thus became fully fruitful in Naciketas.

त्रिणाचिकेतस्त्रिभिरेत्य सन्धिं
त्रिकर्मकृत् तरति जन्ममृत्यू ।
ब्रह्मजज्ञं देवमीड्यं विदित्वा
निचाय्येमां शान्तिमत्यन्तमेति ॥ १७ ॥

triṇāciketas tribhir etya sandhiṁ
trikarmakṛt tarati janma-mṛtyū ।
brahmaja-jñaṁ devam īḍyaṁ viditvā
nicāyyemām śāntiṁ atyantam eti ॥ 17 ॥

One, having lit the Nāciketa fire thrice, associating oneself with the three (father, mother and teacher), who performs the three acts (*yajña*, *dāna* and *tapas*), crosses over birth and death. With the adorable god born of *Brahman* known, one obtains this everlasting peace.

Eulogizing the fire-sacrifice just taught, after applauding Naciketas, this verse delineates the benefit that accrues to one who understands and practises it. The realm of wisdom has not yet been entered. The crossing over of birth and death and the attaining of the everlasting peace referred to here are to be understood therefore as they are relevant to the Vedic context of ritual, and are supposedly experienced by those who have reached heaven.

Performing the fire-sacrifice three times a day (*triṇāciketa*) is customary among those who strictly adhere to the ritualistic cult. The word could also be understood more philosophically, to mean any person in whom the instruction of the fire-sascrifice has taken root through learning, understanding and practice. Whoever accomplishes these three aspects, considering it a binding duty, is called *trikarma-kṛt* (one who has performed the three acts). *Trikarma-kṛt* in the context of ritual means, one who observes the three pious deeds: *yajña* (fire-sacrifice), *dāna* (giving away gifts), *tapas* (observing austerity and self-restraint). The everlasting peace is qualified as *imām śāntim* (this particular peace) suggesting its conditional nature. The god thus known is termed *brahmaja* (one who is born of *Brahman*) and not *Brahman* itself. Knowledge of *Brahman* is reserved for the wisdom teaching that ensues.

त्रिणाचिकेतस्त्रयमेतद् विदित्वा
य एवं विद्वांश्चिनुते नाचिकेतम् ।
स मृत्युपाशान् पुरतः प्रणोद्य
शोकातिगो मोदते स्वर्गलोके ।। १८ ।।

triṇāciketas trayam etad viditvā
ya evaṁ vidvāṁś cinute nāciketam ।
sa mṛtyu-pāśān purataḥ praṇodya
śokātigo modate svargaloke ।। 18 ।।

The wise one who, knowing these three factors, raises the Naciketa fire thrice a day, casts off the snares of death first and going beyond sorrows, rejoices in heaven.

The highest happiness one could expect entailing ritual is that of rejoicing in heaven.

एष तेऽग्निर्नचिकेतः स्वर्ग्यो
यमवृणीथा द्वितीयेन वरेण ।
एतमग्निं तवैव प्रवक्ष्यन्ति जनास-
स्तृतीयं वरं नचिकेतो वृणीष्व ।। १९ ।।

eṣa te'gnir naciketaḥ svargyo
yam avṛṇīthā dvitīyena vareṇa ।
etam agniṁ tava iva pravakṣyanti janāsas-
tṛtīyaṁ varam naciketo vṛṇīṣva ।। 19 ।।

O Naciketas, that knowledge of the heaven-leading sacrifical fire that you chose as your second boon, is already yours. This fire, people will speak of by your name only. Now choose your third boon.

येयं प्रेते विचिकित्सा मनुष्ये-
ऽस्तीत्येके नायमस्तीति चैके ।
एतद् विद्यामनुशिष्टस्त्वयाहं
वराणामेष वरस्तृतीयः ।। २० ।।

yeyaṁ prete vicikitsā manuṣye-
'stītyeke nāyam astīti caike ।

etad vidyām anuśiṣṭas tvayāhaṁ
varāṇām eṣa varas tṛtīyaḥ ॥ 20 ॥

This uncertainty remains among men concerning the departed: some say (the departed) continue to exist; some say they do not. I, taught by you, would like to know, its (truth). Of the boons, I choose this as the third.

The fundamental problem to be dealt with in this Upaniṣad is the one that has been tormenting man ever since he began to think of life — the problem of death and the state after death. This knowledge is the third boon Naciketas chooses. The God of Death, knowing full well that it is no easy task, admits in the next verse the uniqueness of the problem and the uncertainty about it prevailing even among gods.

देवैरत्रापि विचिकित्सितं पुरा
न हि सुज्ञेयमणुरेष धर्मः ।
अन्यं वरं नचिकेतो वृणीष्व
मा मोपरोत्सीरति मा सृजैनम् ॥ २१ ॥

devair atrāpi vicikitsitaṁ purā
na hi sujñeyam aṇur eṣa dharmaḥ ।
anyaṁ varaṁ naciketo vṛṇīsva
mā moparotsīr ati mā sṛjainam ॥ 21 ॥

(Yama said:) Even the gods of old had doubt on this point. It is not, indeed, easy to understand; so subtle is this sustaining truth. O Naciketas, choose another boon. Do not press me. Give up this one for my sake.

By admitting how difficult a question it is, Yama is also testing how fit Naciketas is to receive this noble and subtle wisdom. A problem that confounded even the gods, how is it to be understood by a human being, that too a boy ! Is this boy ingeneous enough to go into the depth of the problem? Is his thirst for this knowledge indefatigable? A Guru, before beginning his teaching, has to ascertain all these. So Yama asks him to choose another boon, knowing that if Naciketas's yearning is not intense enough he would take heed of this suggestion, and choose another boon instead.

देवैरत्रापि विचिकित्सितं किल
त्वं च मृत्यो यन्न सुज्ञेयमात्थ ।
वक्ता चास्य त्वादृगन्यो न लभ्यो
नान्यो वरस्तुल्य एतस्य कश्चित् ।। २२ ।।

devair atrāpi vicikitsitaṁ kila
tvaṁ ca mṛtyo yan na sujñeyam āttha ।
vaktā cāsya tvādṛg anyo na labhyo
nānyo varas tulya etasya kaścit ।। 22 ।।

(Naciketas said:) That even gods have doubts as to this, you yourself say, O Death, and that it is not easy to comprehend. No better teacher than you therefore is available; no better boon to choose either.

The words of Yama, discouraging as they look, convinces Naciketas that the teacher he approached is the right Guru (*sad-guru*). That he (Death) knows what the gods of old had doubts about and his knowing that this sustaining truth is not easily comprehended is clear indication that he knows what the secret is. Naciketas's words, 'No better boon to choose' show how focussed his quest for wisdom is; no one can dissuade him from it. That he is fully endowed with all the other qualities essential in a true seeker (*sat śiṣya*) becomes evident in the coming verses.

शतायुषः पुत्रपौत्रान् वृणीष्व
बहून् पशून् हस्तिहिरण्यमश्वान् ।
भूमेर्महदायतनं वृणीष्व
स्वयं च जीव शरदो यावदिच्छसि ।। २३ ।।

śatāyuṣaḥ putra-pautrān vṛṇīṣva
bahūn paśūn hasti-hiraṇyam aśvān ।
bhūmer mahad-āyatanaṁ vṛṇīṣva
svayaṁ ca jīva śarado yāvad icchasi ।। 23 ।।

(Yama said:) Choose children and grandchildren of a hundred years' life, cattle in plenty, elephants, gold and horses. Choose extensive land and life for yourself as many years as you will.

एतत्तुल्यं यदि मन्यसे वरं
वृणीष्व वित्तं चिरजीविकां च ।
महाभूमौ नचिकेतस्त्वमेधि
कामानां त्वा कामभाजं करोमि ।। २४ ।।

etat tulyaṁ yadi manyase varaṁ
vṛṇīṣva vittaṁ cira-jīvikāṁ ca ।
mahābhūmau naciketas tvam edhi
kāmānāṁ tvā kāma-bhājaṁ karomi ।। 24 ।।

If you think of some other boon equally good, wealth or long life, choose it. O Naciketas, prosper thus on this vast region. I shall make you the enjoyer of all such desires.

ये ये कामा दुर्लभा मर्त्यलोके
सर्वान् कामांश्छन्दतः प्रार्थयस्व ।
इमा रामाः सरथाः सतूर्या
न हीदृशा लभ्यनीया मनुष्यैः ।।
आभिर्मत्प्रत्ताभिः परिचारयस्व
नचिकेतो मरणं मानुप्राक्षीः ।। २५ ।।

ye ye kāmā durlabhā martyaloke
sarvān kāmāṁś chandataḥ prārthayasva ।
imā rāmāḥ sarathāḥ satūryā
nahīdṛśā labhyanīyā manuṣyaiḥ ।
ābhir mat prattābhiḥ paricārayasva
naciketo maraṇaṁ mānuprākṣīḥ ।। 25 ।।

Whatever the desirable things hard to attain in this world of mortals, ask for them as you choose. Here are charming young women along with chariots and musical instruments, the like of which is hardly obtainable to men. Be served by them whom I give you. But, O Naciketas, do not seek to know about death.

Offering still more worldly attractions — a happy family life with long-living children and grand-children, wealth, gold, young women, elephants, horses, even to be the overlord of an extensive region, the highest position one could aspire after in worldly life — Yama tries to rouse in Naciketas the zest for pleasure, but he, unrelenting, says:

श्वोभावा मर्त्यस्य यदन्तकैतत्
सर्वेन्द्रियाणां जरयन्ति तेजः ।
अपि सर्वं जीवितमल्पमेव
तवैव वाहास्तव नृत्यगीते ।। २६ ।।

śvobhāvā martyasya yad antakaitat
sarvendriyāṇāṁ jarayanti tejaḥ ।
api sarvaṁ jīvitam alpam eva
tavaiva vāhās tava nṛtya-gīte ।। 26 ।।

(Naciketas said:) O End-maker, ephemeral as all these are, they wear out the vigour of every sense of the mortal (man). All life is short indeed. Yours be the chariots, yours be the dance and music.

When Naciketas speaks it becomes clear that he has no interest in any of the pleasures offered by Yama. Yama is addressed as *antaka*, which means the End-maker. The real end-maker of all beings as well as the originator, is none but the Absolute, the one Reality underlying all appearances. Yama as a Guru represents that Reality. How a Guru and the Absolute of which he teaches are one, will become clear as we proceed. Naciketas, who proves his genius, by the next verse, stands out as a genuine seeker of the highest order, known as *uttama adhikārī*; the one of the middle grade being *madhyama adhikārī*, and the one of low grade, *manda-adhikārī*.

न वित्तेन तर्पणीयो मनुष्यो
लप्स्यामहे वित्तमद्राक्ष्म चेत्त्वा ।
जीविष्यामो यावदीशिष्यसि त्वं
वरस्तु मे वरणीयः स एव ।। २७ ।।

na vittena tarpaṇīyo manuṣyo
lapsyāmahe vittam adrākṣma cetvā ।
jīviṣyāmo yāvad īśiṣyasi tvaṁ
varas tu me varaṇīyaḥ sa eva ।। 27 ।।

> Man is not satisfied with wealth alone. Now that we have met you, we'll get all the wealth we need. We'll live as you will. So the only boon worth choosing is the one already chosen.

Naciketas's lack of interest in worldly pleasures has already been revealed. He relinquishes them, not for the sake of relinquishing. Wealth and long life by themselves are not undesirable values. But man does not find satisfaction in them alone; he feels unsatisfied even on attaining wealth. Had Nachiketas chosen the wealth offered by Yama, he would have got that alone, nothing more. But the boon chosen by Naciketas ensures the highest wisdom which brings about unasked all worldly necessities. But acquiring this wisdom needs the grace of a Guru, and therefore, as far as the seeker is concerned, meeting a real Guru is the greatest wealth, which Naciketas is now blessed with.

Whether one desires long life or not, one's life-span is always dictated by Death who is already with Naciketas willing to grant anything. As is observed, the worldly needs of those who are dedicated to wisdom are somehow provided by the Absolute. Possessing wisdom, therefore, means possessing everything.

अजीर्यताममृतानामुपेत्य
जीर्यन्मर्त्यः क्वधः स्थः प्रजानन् ।
अभिध्यायन्वर्णरतिप्रमोदा-
नतिदीर्घे जीविते को रमेत ॥ २८ ॥

ajīryatām amṛtānām upetya
jīryan martyaḥ kvadhaḥ sthaḥ prajānan ।
abhidhyāyan varṇa-rati-pramodān
atidīrghe jīvite ko rameta ॥ 28 ॥

> Having approached the undecaying state of the immortals, which mortal, aware of and deliberating on the (nature) of pleasures of beauty and love, will find joy in an over-long life?

There is no better teacher of the secret of death than the Death himself. Death is deathless, is immortal (*amṛta*). The Guru, Naciketas has chosen, is immortal Death. In principle, the Guru is birthless and deathless. If someone is asked to choose a boon, he should choose the best that the particular situation offers. For a mortal (*martya*, literally the mortal, meaning man) in the abode of an immortal, especially for a seeker of the order of Naciketas, the best thing he could ask for is immortality. He, therefore, instead of asking for an over-long life, asks for immortality!

यस्मिन्निदं विचिकित्सन्ति मृत्यो
यत् साम्पराये महति ब्रूहि नस्तत् ।
योऽयं वरो गूढमनुप्रविष्टो
नान्यं तस्मान्नचिकेता वृणीते ॥ २९ ॥

yasminnidaṁ vicikitsanti mṛtyo
yat sāmparāye mahati brūhi nas tat ।
yo'yaṁ varo gūḍham anupraviṣṭho
nānyaṁ tasmān naciketā vṛṇīte ॥ 29 ॥

O Death, tell me of the beyond about which there has been much doubt prevailing — the knowledge which is followed by great results. Apart from this knowledge that penetrates the mystery, no other boon does this Naciketas choose.

Fully aware of the confusion that surrounds the problem and of the uncertainty even gods still have about it, Naciketas holds firmly on to his boon.

The stage is thus all set for the real wisdom dialogue to begin between the Immortal Death and the unrelenting Naciketas. The ultimate benefit of the teaching is attainment of Immortality, not for Naciketas alone, but for all of us seekers too.

Chapter II

द्वितीया वल्ली

अन्यच्छ्रेयोऽन्यदुतैव प्रेय-
स्ते उभे नानार्थे पुरुषं सिनीतः ।
तयोः श्रेय आददानस्य साधु
भवति हीयतेऽर्थाद्य उ प्रेयो वृणीते ।। १ ।।

anyat śreyo'nyad utaiva preyas-
te ubhe nānārthe puruṣaṁ sinītaḥ ।
tayoḥ śreya ādadānasya sādhu
bhavati hīyate'rthād ya u preyo vṛṇīte ।। 1 ।।

(Yama said:) That which is of the highest value (*śreyas*) is one; that which is pleasant here and now (*preyas*) is another. Serving different purposes, the two make men blind. Of the two, well is it for him who chooses *śreyas*. He fails his aim who chooses *preyas*.

THE wisdom dialogue proper begins with an evaluation of our value notions. One characteristic distinguishes human life from animal life: animals simply live, but man leads his life. To lead life one has to have an end in view, and man's value notions decide this end. This set of value notions, different for each person, could in a general way be classified into two: *śreyas* and *preyas*.

To own a beautiful and comfortable house with as many objects of enjoyment and convenience as possible, to have a healthy body with a long life, to have a good reputation and reputable children and the like, are the values coveted by most people. Such values of a worldly nature constitute *preyas*, literally, the beloved, more agreeable.

There are people, albeit a few, who feel that knowing the meaning of life, and realizing it while living, is what makes life meaningful. They, being engrossed in this one master interest, don't care much for the other. Just as stars get dimmed and finally disappear as the Sun rises, so the interest in worldly matters become insignificant on the dawning of the quest for Reality. This value notion which Naciketas is guided by, is *śreyas*, literally, the superior, the dearer, the blessed, the final Blissfulness.

Whatever one chooses, *preyas* or *śreyas*, one feels committed to it, and bound by it. Being bound by *śreyas* brings in final release from all bondages, and so is it considered *sādhu* (good, superior, valid). Being committed to *preyas*, unaware of the real meaning of life, on the contrary, one is deprived of a human life. Yama, fully approving Naciketas's value discrimination, compliments him.

श्रेयश्च प्रेयश्च मनुष्यमेत-
स्तौ सम्परीत्य विविनक्ति धीरः ।
श्रेयो हि धीरोऽभि प्रेयसो वृणीते
प्रेयो मन्दो योगक्षेमाद् वृणीते ।। २ ।।

sreyaś ca preyaś ca manuṣyam etas-
tau samparītya vivinakti dhīraḥ ।
śreyo hi dhīro'bhi preyaso vṛṇīte
preyo mando yogo-kṣemād vṛṇīte ।। 2 ।।

Both *śreyas* and *preyas* approach man. The wise, fully surveying them, discriminates and chooses *śreyas* in preference to *preyas*. The stupid, interested in worldly well-being, chooses *preyas*.

Śreyas and *preyas* — figuratively personified — approach man to be accepted by him, instead of his searching for them, implying that such possibilities appear in practical life quite naturally and abundantly. Man is free to choose, with the guidance only of his own value notions. The word *manuṣya*, meaning man, literally the progeny of Manu — one who thinks — is especially significant, for what makes man formutlate his value notions and determine what he prefers is his thinking. To discriminate good and evil, right and wrong, is a sign of thought.

Though the entire range of value experiences, from the most elementary pleasures to the sublimest one of higher wisdom, present themselves to be wooed, one need not accept them all; one has to be discriminative. The wise one, not bewitched by *preyas*, chooses *śreyas*, as Naciketas did. Such a person of resoluteness is to be called *dhīra*, literally one who shares knowledge with others, in common usage, a person of firmness. The yearning for *preyas*, he feels, is a sort of obstacle to freedom, *mukti* or *mokṣa*, the highest value he aims at.

If *preyas* and *śreyas* present themselves before man to be chosen, it could be asked, "Why is it that many live indigent and fully ignorant of higher values?"

Whether one is infused with a sense of higher values or not is seldom made out. Illiterate old women living in shacks in remote hamlets of India could be found to be brimming with the spirit of wisdom, untaught. Their worldly indigence does not make their inner richness any less.

There do come those, though rare, who, with an inner urge for making life meaningful, studiedly choose the path of *śreyas*, and there are others who do not care in the least for it. How rare the *śreyas*-seekers are is emphatically stated in the *Bhagavad Gītā* thus:

> One perchance among thousands strive for this attainment; and even among thousands of such attainers, perchance one knows Me truly. (VII.3)

Śreyas always shows itself; one has to be discriminate enough to recognize it and choose it.

Always urged by the instinct for self-preservation and enjoyment as he is, man requires no special prodding to make him choose *preyas*. Man's most instinctive cravings are for wife or husband (*dāreṣaṇā*), for one's children (*putreṣaṇā*), for one's wealth (*vitteṣaṇā*), together called the *esaṇā- traya* (triple cravings). It is not that these are uncommendable human values, but elevating them beyond limit, so that they become a hindrance to one's own freedom, is equal to violating the human nature in us. If one desires freedom one has to free oneself from the captivating embrace of instinctive cravings. Though worldly values are said to offer themselves to all, in practice they are not accessible to many. Nature offers such joys to everyone as part of its self-unfoldment. What man, a part of nature's self-unfoldment, has to do is to enjoy them as every other living being does. Possessing those enjoyable things as one's own, based on the man-made law of private property, goes against the God-made law of nature. This disparity between two kinds of laws is piquantly exposed by the *ṛṣi* of the *Īśa Upaniṣad* when he asks, "Whose is wealth?" (*kasya svid dhanam*). It is of none; it is God's; man has right only to enjoy them. Once man-made laws are formulated fully honouring the God-made laws, the present problem could be expected to be solved. Till then the present striving for social justice must continue. Are those who clamour for human rights, willing to forgo the possessions they grabbed violating all God-made laws?

स त्वं प्रियान् प्रियरूपांश्च कामा-
नभिध्यायन् नचिकेतोऽत्यस्राक्षीः ।
नैतां सृङ्कां वित्तमयीमवाप्तो
यस्यां मज्जन्ति बहवो मनुष्याः ।। ३ ।।

sa tvaṁ priyān priyarūpāṁś ca kāmān
abhidhyāyan naciketo'tyasrākṣīḥ ।
naitāṁ sṛṅkāṁ vittamayīm avāpto
yasyāṁ majjanti bahavo manuṣyāḥ ।। 3 ।।

O Naciketas, you, being such, when pleasant and beautiful desirables presented themselves, rightly reflecting on, have rejected them. You did not choose the garland of wealth that chains you up. Many are who sink therein.

Yama continues his compliments:

Something could be considered desirable for either its use value or its aesthetic value. What Yama had offered Naciketas was a royal life matchless in both respects. Attractive though they are, such gladly accepted gains are like garlands that chain you up.

दूरमेते विपरीते विषूची
अविद्या या च विद्येति ज्ञाता ।
विद्याभीप्सिनं नचिकेतसं मन्ये
न त्वा कामा बहवोऽलोलुपन्त ।। ४ ।।

dūram ete viparīte viṣūcī
avidyā yā ca vidyeti jñātā ।
vidyābhīpsinaṁ naciketasaṁ manye
na tvā kāmā bahavo'lolupanta ॥ 4 ॥

Widely apart and leading to divergent ends are indeed what are known as ignorance (*avidyā*) and knowledge (*vidyā*). That Naciketas is eager for knowledge I realize, for many a desirable tempted you not.

A new set of dual concepts, *vidyā* and *avidyā*, are introduced here, as means to the ends of *śreyas* and *preyas*. It is not everybody who is capable to discriminating and choosing between the two. The discriminating ones always choose *śreyas*. *Vidyā* is its means. Others, not even aware of the choice available, take to the way of *preyas*. *Avidyā* is that which veils the need for discrimination and choice, making those under its spell take *preyas* for *śreyas*. There are also a few who are discriminative, but are not resolute enough to take to *śreyas*. Always feeling caught in between the devil and the deep sea, they curse themselves; they are also sunk in *avidyā*.

Sri Narayana Guru defines *vidyā* as,

> That because of which the Self (the Real) looms as real and the non-Self (the unreal)as unreal is *vidyā*, as is rope understood as real and the snake as the unreal superimposed on the rope.

And *avidyā* as,

> That because of which the non-Self (the unreal) looms as real, and the Self (the Real) as unreal is *avidyā* indeed, as the erroneous cognition of rope as snake.
>
> (*Darśanamālā*, IV.3, 4)

Even reasoning, a mode of the very same *avidyā*, does not help one erase it and therefore *avidyā* is difficult to cross over (*viṣūcī*).

अविद्यायामन्तरे वर्तमानाः
स्वयं धीराः पण्डितंमन्यमानाः ।
दन्द्रम्यमाणाः परियन्ति मूढा
अन्धेनैव नीयमाना यथान्धाः ॥ ५ ॥

avidyāyāṁ antare vartamānāḥ
svayaṁ dhīrāḥ paṇḍitaṁ manyamānāḥ ।
dandramyamāṇāḥ pariyanti mūḍhā
andhen aiva nīyamānā yathāndhāḥ ॥ 5 ॥

Abiding in the midst of ignorance, wise in their own esteem, considering themselves learned, fools there are, running around taking to crooked ways, like the blind guiding the blind.

There are those who are learned, and there also are those who believe themselves to be learned but really are not. The former are called *paṇḍitāḥ* and the latter *paṇḍitammanyāḥ*. Perhaps, due to lack of guidance, unable to find their true identity, the latter take to wrong paths in life, unfit to their own inner nature. This eventually ends up in the personality aberration of becoming rigidly fixed, and thus leading their lives unheeding others. Such characters are called *svayam dhīrāḥ* (wise in their own esteem). They will have no hesitation in teaching others and guiding others, like a blind person leading another equally blind.

People toil in far off lands, even in deserts and mid-seas, to make money in the hope of having a future happy life. They, while toiling thus, do not feel as if they are living, but feel instead as if preparing for living. This preparation goes on and on until the day comes when they feel no more of that life is before them. They thus die without having really lived, all this the result of ignorance. They didn't remember that life is to be lived in the present and not in the future. The way of transforming the same life into a real feeling of living in the present is cleared open by the wisdom taught in Upaniṣads like this one. This feeling of really living does not terminate even with the termination of the individual entity called 'I'. What is real in 'me' continues to exist, living immortally, even after the entity called 'I' disappears. Life is an eternal and infinite unfoldment of an unfathomable creativity inherent in what is Real, the Self, *Brahman*. Such is the nature of wisdom about to be revealed to Naciketas. Those who are unaware of it, and those who do not care for it, always afraid of death, go straight to death, as we see in the next verse.

न साम्परायः प्रतिभाति बालं
प्रमाद्यन्तं वित्तमोहेन मूढम् ।
अयं लोको नास्ति पर इति मानी
पुनः पुनर्वशमापद्यते मे ॥ ६ ॥

na sāmparāyaḥ pratibhāti bālaṁ
pramādyantaṁ vitta-mohena mūḍham ।
ayaṁ loko nāsti para iti mānī
punaḥ punar vaśam āpadyate me ॥ 6 ॥

The beyond is not visible to the ignorant, heedless, deluded by the glamour of wealth. Thinking, 'This world is what exists, nothing beyond', again and again he reaches me (death).

Naciketas desired to be taught the secret of death, that phenomenon which arouses great anxiety and fear in life. Fully aware of the inevitability of death though, we try to avoid it at any cost. Birth is its other pole. The birth of a child is a jubilant event for parents. They consider it as making their life meaningful. Yet they remain ignorant of the one ever existing Substance that unfolds itself as the birth, life-span and death of each and every being, and therefore ignorant of one's oneness with that Substance.

Used to the habit of thinking what we perceive with our senses as real, phenomenal birth and death are also taken to be real; with the result that there is fear of death and jubilation over birth. Considering birth and death as marking the beginning and end of life, we try to make what is in between as pleasant as possible, accumulating wealth and collecting all sorts of enjoyables. This deluded concept of life is called *moha* where one is incapable of distinguishing the real from the unreal, the right from the wrong. To those in its spell it does not occur that a brithless and deathless Reality exists underneath all these appearances, and that one's identity with it, immortality, is realizable; they are to be called *mūḍhas* (fools, ignoramouses). For them birth is real, death is real, the cycle of birth and death is real; what ensues is the feeling: the world is an ocean of sufferings despite all the pleasurable objects acquired.

The problem of the hereafter torments only the minds of those who take death as real. To those who know that the real Substance in one's own existence transcends birth and death, the problem of the state after death does not arise at all. The question asked by Naciketas arose from the delusion of taking appearance as reality. Once free of this delusion (*bhrama*), one attains the certitude of the Real (*pramā*), and conversely, once the Real is understood one becomes free of this delusion. Yama's attempt in this Upaniṣad is to teach the immortality of one's Self, of oneself.

श्रवणायापि बहुभिर्यो न लभ्यः
श्रृण्वन्तोऽपि बहवो यं न विद्युः ।
आश्चर्यो वक्ता कुशलोऽस्य लब्धा-
ऽऽश्चर्यो ज्ञाता कुशलानुशिष्टः ।। ७ ।।

śrvaṇāyāpi bahubhir yo na labhyaḥ
śr̥ṇvanto'pi bahavo yaṁ na vidyuḥ ।
āścaryo vaktā kuśalo'sya labdhā
āścaryo jñātā kuśal ānuśiṣṭaḥ ।। 7 ।।

Unavailable for many is it even for learning. Not understood by many is it even after learning. Its expounder is a mystery, its receiver happy and prosperous. Its knower, well-taught, too is a mystery.

Solving the problem of the state after death, by realizing the deathless Reality one already is, is possible only for those who give up the habitual idea that what is apparent is the Real. They turn their attention — a turning point in life — to the changeless Reality underlying all changing states. Even being fully interested in knowing that Reality need not necessarily help one to clear the path to it. Intellectual acumen and a critical attitude being of no avail in this respect, as we shall see shortly, the guidance of a person who has already attained it becomes essential in reaching this goal. One need not necessarily find a Guru simply because one is in search of a guide. The thirst for wisdom and meeting a real guide is a strange coincidence, willed as it were by Providence.

Becoming inquisitive and having the good fortune to meet a proper Guru alone do not ensure the final attainment, which always depends on how competent the disciple is. How long a seeker would have to be with the Guru before the real teaching takes place, also varies according to the seeker's competence. The teaching may take place immediately, or the seeker may have to stay with the Guru for years — one, three, six, twelve — or even a whole lifetime. Still it may happen that the seeker does not get into the core of the teaching, even after being taught, after all the waiting.

The intimacy that is established between the Guru and the seeker is one of the most important factors and plays a crucial role in determining the fruitfulness of the wisdom teaching. What the Guru is aware of and intends to pass on to the disciple is the essential content of *his* existence. What the disciple is in search of is the essential content of *his* own existence. The Guru through his teaching reveals *his* self-awareness, and the disciple has to imbibe it as *his* own. This transformation of one's intimate personal experience into another's requires a personal intimacy between the two.

The thirst for wisdom, the fitness to receive wisdom, the bipolarity established with the Guru, these three are thus essential prerequisites. In the absence of any one, the words of teaching, if at all the teaching takes place, just pass overhead. Hearing with full attention, the seeker on his part has to ponder over what has been heard (*manana*), followed by meditation (*nididhyāsana*); only then will the meaning of what was taught really dawn on him. The secret of wisdom, therefore it is said, is not understood by many even on hearing or learning.

The experience of one who knows Reality, is the subjectless, objectless awareness of self-existence. The seeker becoming a seer is a mystery. The Reality thus seen is a mystery. Knowing it is a mystery, the knower of it too is a mystery.

Life, as visualized by a *jñānin*, man of wisdom, is the incessant flow of the creative self-expression of what is Real, the Self, and not an ocean of suffering. What we call pleasure and pain are merely the self-expressions of the *ānanda* content of the Self. This life, pulsating in the entire range of existence, from the subatomic to the cosmic, from mental to physical, is eternal and what exists in and appears as all these, is immortal. The seer experiences himself as a drop in the ocean of that eternal and infinite existence. In this experience of immortality he finds himself well provided for by the same Reality: a state of well-being and blissfulness called *kuśala*.

न नरेणावरेण प्रोक्त एष
सुविज्ञेयो बहुधा चिन्त्यमानः ।
अनन्यप्रोक्ते गतिरत्र नास्त्य-
णीयान् ह्यतर्क्यमणुप्रमाणात् ॥ ८ ॥

na nareṇāvareṇa prokta eṣa
suvijñeyo bahudhā cintyamānaḥ ।
ananya-prokte gatir atra nāsti
aṇīyān hi atarkyam aṇu-pramāṇāt ॥ 8 ॥

Thought of variously, It (the Self) is not truely understood, taught by an inferior person. When taught by the one who sees himself not different from the Real, then no other goal remains to attain. For, subtler than the subtlest, it is inaccessible to reasoning.

Scientists and thinkers, in the search for the reality which underlies the apparent, through experiments and calculations, and ratiocinative thinking respectively, have mind alone for their tool, which they use variously to arrive at various conclusions concerning one reality. There are thinkers who consider sense-perception the most dependable means of knowledge, those who think ratiocination to be the most reliable, and those who look for what is beyond the grasp of the reasoning mind, through intuition. Each school of thought has its own vision of truth, and each is a facet of the truth, arrived at through thinking conditioned by the preferred method of approach, the means of certitude relied on, the accepted basic premises and pre-conceptions. For instance, the search for reality conditioned by the pre-conception that matter is the cause of everything, will not and cannot arrive at a conclusion about anything more than the material aspect of reality. Though none of such conclusions is wrong, none is final and complete. Even as the altercation for and against such conclusions goes on, reality, their main concern, remains unconcerned. Narayana Guru sheds light on this oddity in his *Ātmopadeśa Śatakam* as follows:

The bottom is real, and top is real, the end is real;
that is real, this is real, yet another is real;
altercation thus prevails, whilst the primordial
reality is all that is.

(Verse 19)

To have such parochial views of reality is inferior (*avaram*) to the holistic vision. The teaching on reality, imparted by one of incomplete vision, though intellectually perfect and convincing, would never help in visualizing reality in its entirety and purity.

The real knower of Truth is he who finds his oneness with It, just as an ornament is inseparably one with gold. Taught by such a man of attainment, the seeker also finds identification with what is real in him, the Self, *ātman*. Then he finds his search has reached its finale, no further to go and no other goal to reach.

Accustomed to thinking of things in terms of quantity, as big or small, long or short, heavy or light, one might be prone to think of the Self also in such terms. Quantitatively speaking, It is smaller than the smallest (*aṇu pramāṇāt aṇīyān*) and bigger than the biggest. *Aṇu*, considered as equivalent to the modern concept of atom, really means, the indivisibly small, and its modern equivalent is the sub-atomic particle. Reaching the lowest level of subatomic existence, the theoretical physicist finds it impossible to say whether it is particle or wave, that is to say, whether it is matter or non-matter. Even in modern physics, thus, as it touches the subtlest level of existence, reality, till then understood quantitatively, attains a qualitative dimension, adding to the mystery. The *ṛṣi*, however, relying only on intuitive vision, and perceiving that reality is a great mystery, put the whole thing in qualitative terms, saying, "subtler than the subtlest and greater than the greatest". This reality, *ātman*, is consciousness (*cit*) in essence. All the ideas such as big and small, good and bad, get formulated in *cit*, which in itself is neither big nor small, neither good nor bad.

To claim that something is smaller than the smallest and bigger than the biggest, logically speaking, is contradictory and therefore untenable. All logic is based on the principle of causality. That differentiating cause and effect is an artifact of human reasoning and it in no way affects the unity of the entity or fact theorized on, is a fact that most of us are oblivious to. Establishing, for example, that clay is the cause of the pot in no way separates pot from clay; they remain inseparably one, though theoretically differentiated as cause and effect. The primal source of the cause-effect duality, and therefore, of all ratiocination, being *cit*, no reasoning helps in ascertaining what that *cit* is, and so it is *atarkya* (inaccessible to reasoning).

नैषा तर्केण मतिरापनेया
प्रोक्तान्येनैव सुज्ञानाय प्रेष्ठ ।
यां त्वमापः सत्यधृतिर्बतासि
त्वादृङ् नो भूयान्नचिकेतः प्रष्टा ।। ९ ।।

naiṣā tarkeṇa matir āpaneyā
proktānyenaiva sujñānāya preṣṭha ।
yāṁ tvam āpaḥ satya-dhṛtir batāsi
tvādṛṅ no bhūyān naciketaḥ praṣṭā ।। 9 ।।

Not by reasoning is this wisdom attainable; but, O Dearest, taught otherwise is it well understood. Holding fast to Truth, you have attained it. May our seekers be like you, O Naciketas.

Search of any kind for reality is a mental activity, reasoning a part of it. Logical reasoning begins from a minor premise, as known to everyone. It passes through a middle term and more postulates, and finally comes to a conclusion. Since no such minor premise is available of the Self and therefore the Absolute, no reasoning about it is possible. Reasoning, thus whether of the teacher or the taught, does not help one attain the Absolute. Yama, in this wisdom discourse, also does not try to prove logically what he teaches. He, as a seer, just verbally reveals the Truth which, he realizes, is not different from himself, making Naciketas also visualize Truth as his own self-being. We, the students of the Upaniṣad, are also expected to find the core of its teaching not through reasoning.

Naciketas, steadfast and uncompromising in his quest for Truth, is at Its doorway. The wisdom, about to be imparted to him, should not be lost to posterity. To receive it and to hand it down to future generations, seekers of Naciketas's calibre have to emerge from time to time. Yama, therefore, wishes for more worthy seekers.

The word *naḥ* (ours) used by Yama studiedly brackets Naciketas with him; Naciketas, Yama hopes, would be instrumental in handing this wisdom down to similar seekers in future.

जानाम्यहं शेवधिरित्यनित्यं
न ह्यध्रुवैः प्राप्यते हि ध्रुवं तत् ।
ततो मया नाचिकेतश्चितोऽग्नि-
रनित्यैर्द्रव्यैः प्राप्तवानस्मि नित्यम् ।। १० ।।

jānāmy ahaṁ śevadhir ityanityaṁ
na hyadhruvaiḥ prāpyate hi dhruvaṁ tat ।
tato mayā nāciketaś cito'gniḥ
anityair dravyaiḥ prāptavān asmi nityam ॥ 10 ॥

This treasure, I am aware, is transient, and by transient means that eternal is unattainable indeed. I still pile up the Nāciketa sacrificial fire with transient things, and I do attain the eternal.

Yama knows what is eternally Real and what is the meaning of transient appearance of which, wealth and pleasurable objects are a part. Those who consider the latter as of high value are unaware of the eternal value of Reality underlying everything. Yama, well founded in wisdom, knows that the eternal Reality finds self-expression in the form of transient entities. The realization of Reality must therefore be accomplished with the transient as the means, even as eternal gold is seen in and through the transient forms of ornaments. The transient world is eternally active and eternally changing, whilst the eternal Reality remains unchanged. The *jñānin* sees one eternal Reality alone in all apparent forms, their actions and changefulness. With such a view of life Yama still continues to be active in the world of transient values, symbolized by his continued kindling of the sacrificial fire. Such is the way a *jñānin* lives in this world. He too, like everyone else, lives in this transient world, involved in activities natural to him as part of the functional system of the one eternal Reality; his duty as the God of Death, his living in a palace with servants and all the accompanying paraphernalia, are all a part of it. While in the midst of all this he remains unattached. Even his teaching Naciketas, is part of that kindling of the Nāciketa fire, symbolically suggesting the kindling of the perennial wisdom in the transient Naciketas for transmission to other transient beings like him. The spirit of this stanza is well brought out in the *Bhagavad Gītā*:

In the three worlds there is no
action which I need do, O Partha,
nor is there for Me anything
worth attaining unattained;
even so I am engaged in action.

(III. 22)

Naciketas is still a seeker. What is of prime import for him is the method of seeking, where ignoring the transient to attain the eternal is quite natural, whereas a *jñānin* sees the eternal alone in all that is transient. Ignoring the worldly affairs is thus not part of the Vedāntic doctrine, but is only a methodological necessity on the part of a seeker.

It is esential to distinguish the stage where the seeker is and the one the man of attainment has reached. The former is ascending from the apparent to the real, the latter, finding himself one with the Real, looks at appearances from above, as it were, and sees them inseparable from the Real and thus from him self. He visualizes the Real as existing in the form of the world.

A Zen story depicts this difference quite clearly: A Zen Guru, on his way with a heavy load on his back, was asked, "How can the Real be known?" He dropped the load and smiled. The questioner asked again: "How is it to be realized?" The Guru put on the load back and walked away.

कामस्याप्तिं जगतः प्रतिष्ठां
क्रतोरानन्त्यमभयस्य पारम् ।
स्तोमं महदुरुगायं प्रतिष्ठां दृष्ट्वा
धृत्या धीरो नचिकेतोऽत्यस्राक्षीः ।। ११ ।।

kāmasyāptiṁ jagataḥ pratiṣṭhāṁ
krator ānantyam abhayasya pāraṁ ।
stomaṁ mahad urugāyaṁ pratiṣṭhāṁ dṛṣṭvā
dhṛtyā dhīro naciketo'tyasrākṣīḥ ।। 11 ।।

The foundation of the world, the best of all desires, the endlessness of sacrifices, the ultimate limit of fearlessness, that which holds within it limitless creativity — having visualized That, you with perseverence have let all else go.

We have seen how Yama, the embodiment of wisdom, views the world of actualities as if from above. Naciketas looking as he is from this world of actualities, birth and death, upwards to the one goal, forgoing all else, is commended in this verse. He, seeing, though vaguely, the prospect of knowing of the state after death, lets go all other attractions and clings to his quest for it which will take him beyond birth and death, to immortality. Seeing himself as the immortal Reality, he also finds that everything desirable is already part of the Self, part of himself. The attainment of the one and final goal includes in it everything already attained and everything yet to attain, and hence there is no need for further search.

Jagat, one of the many words meaning 'the world', literally means that which is constantly moving on, like a flowing river. For the flow to take place, a substance — like water — must be present. The Substance that flows as the world, the foundation of the world, is what Naciketas is aiming to know; knowledge of it alone can solve his problem.

This Substance has inherent in it the endless possibility of actions, resulting in the unceasing emergence of ever new forms, and the merger of old forms. Life thus goes on unceasingly and always new. This overall nature of life is what all the scriptures of the world try to bring home to man in one form or another. This life-pushing force is called *karma*. Admitting life to be so is symbolized by ritual, also called *karma*, sometimes *kratu*, and in all possibility this must have been the origin of ritualism. The possibilites of such ritualistic actions are endless even as the possibilities of actions they symbolize are endless.

Naciketas is still a seeker of wisdom, which until realized remains an unknown yet adorable mystery; once realized it is a known mystery, the knower himself part of it. Naciketas with great expectation is looking forward to its attainment and Yama acknowledges it.

तं दुर्दर्शं गूढमनुप्रविष्टं
गुहाहितं गह्वरेष्ठं पुराणम् ।
अध्यात्मयोगाधिगमेन देवं
मत्वा धीरो हर्षशोकौ जहाति ।। १२ ।।

taṁ durdarśaṁ gūḍham anu-praviṣṭaṁ
guhāhitaṁ gahvareṣṭhaṁ purāṇam ।
adhyātma-yogādhigamena devaṁ
matvā dhīro harṣa-śokau jahāti ।। 12 ।।

Knowing through self-based Yoga-approach that effulgent Existence (*deva*), difficult to perceive, hidden in everything pervading them, set as it were in a cave, pervading even the depth of the cave, the most ancient, one leaves both joy and sorrow behind.

After acknowledging that Naciketas is now ready to enter the sacred realm of wisdom, Yama tells him how secret, enlightening, and beneficial is the wisdom he is going to acquire. The warning that the enquiry is a self-based one (*adhyātma*), and not reason-based, is also implicit in the words. The reality to be realized is in essence pure effulgence and hence a *deva* or god, and the ultimate benefit, leaving both joy and sorrow, birth and death, behind.

Accustomed as we are to seeking reality as if it were an object, we might be tempted to resort to that mode in the present enquiry as well. This reality or *deva*, being the one that subsists everything, including the enquirer and the enquring mind, it can never be reached as an object, yet the enquirer can directly experience it as the substance that pervades his own being. A mind accustomed to exclusively objective enquiry will therefore find this god 'difficult to perceive'.

To intuitively visualize Reality as the essence of one's own being means to visualize the same Reality as the essence of everything that exists. This self-based way of knowing Reality is known as *adhyātma-jñāna*, and being an awareness in which oneself and all things are yoked together, it is *adhyātma-yoga* (*yoga* meaning to yoke). This experience convinces one, oneself — the Self — to be the being in all the specific becomings. Self-existence is an experience of pure effulgence, one then realizes everything in essence is the same effulgence, hidden, but all-pervading.

The figurative imagery of this Self as dwelling in a cave, is very dear to the Upaniṣadic *ṛṣis*. This need not be taken literally, lest it should jeopardize the basic Vedāntic concept that the Self is the substance that assumes the form of all the gross and subtle phenomena of the world. The dark cave simply suggests the impossibility of locating the Self at any particular point. Any enquiry with this latter perspective would be like groping in the dark for the non-existent black cat. Such a possible flaw is immediately corrected by saying, 'it pervades even the depth of the cave', along with the words, 'it is set as it were in a cave'.

Time and space, non-existent by themselves, constitute the warp and the woof of the frame of reference related to which are located in our conscious mind all the events of life. The two are fantasied by our mind for this specific purpose. Time is not an entity, but is the way events are vertically related in terms of continuity; and space, the mental device by which events are related horizontally in terms of contiguity. Events do not take place in time and space, but the two are mental fantasies having bearing on events. In the absence of events, there will neither be time nor space. The Self-Reality, therefore, is not subject to the conditioning of time and space, but time-sense and space-sense have their being in consciousness, the Self. If at all it is to be said how old this Self is, 'It is timeless or the most ancient (*purāṇa*)'.

Consciousness as an experience of effulgence is often personified as *deva* (god), literally the effulgent being, its specific aspects, personified and conceived as presiding over natural phenomena, are the legendary *deva*s (gods), the inhabitants of heaven.

The goal of Vedānta, *ānanda* (experience of self-contentment) is not merely the state of experiencing pleasure. Untouched by pain, rather it is the state in which one goes beyond pleasure and pain and views both with equanimity. Such a person alone can be *dhīra* (firm) in his mind.

एतच्छ्रुत्वा सम्परिगृह्य मर्त्यः।
प्रवृह्य धर्म्यमणुमेतमाप्य ।
स मोदते मोदनीयं हि लब्ध्वा
विवृतं सद्म नचिकेतसं मन्ये ।। १३ ।।

etat śrutvā samparigṛhya martyaḥ
pravṛhya dharmyam aṇum etam āpya ।
sa modate modanīyaṁ hi labdhvā
vivṛtaṁ sadma naciketasaṁ manye ।। 13 ।।

Having heard this and comprehending this, extracting the all-sustaining essence and attaining its subtle secret, man the mortal rejoices on attaining what really makes him happy. That mansion, I feel, is now wide open unto Naciketas.

In Sanskrit, man particularly is called *martya*, meaning the mortal — though all other living beings are also destined to die — as he is the only being who lives constantly afraid of death as if it were lying in wait for him. As a result he is also worried about the state after death. It is this curiosity about the state after death that brought Naciketas to the doorstep of the eternal Reality, which in experiencial terms is eternal Happiness, as we saw in this chapter up to Verse 11. Naciketas's entering this Mansion of wisdom has to be self-based (*adhyātma*), as the next verse shows. On entering, the house is going to become his own home. Knowing Self-Reality is like making the Self one's own home, where one experiences the Absolute Freedom, finding oneself well-established in the Self, identified with the Self. Naciketas is now just about to enter this state. The first step to this entering is proper hearing of the instruction (*śravana*), the second step, comprehending its subtlity through thorough and intensive cogitation (*manana*), and the last step, enjoying oneness through meditation (*nididhyāsana*), all suggested in the present verse, reminiscent of the words of Yājñavalkya to Maitreyi in the *Bṛhadāranyaka Upaniṣad* :

> O Maitreyi, this Self is to be properly heard of, to be properly cogitated on and to be realized in meditation. (IV. 5. 6)

This subtle wisdom Nachiketas is about to gain is also *dharmya*, that which sustains the functional system of the world. *Dhr* means to support, to hold up; the life-supporting principle is *dharma*; that which is worthy of being such a support is *dharmya*.

The rest of the Upaniṣad is Yama's instruction (*upadesa*) on how to enter the mansion, how to comprehend it and how should he find himself one with it like a drop of water getting merged with the flow of an expansive river.

अन्यत्र धर्मादन्यत्राधर्मा-
दन्यत्रास्मात् कृताकृतात् ।
अन्यत्र भूताच्च भव्याच्च
यत्तत्पश्यसि तद्वद ।। १४ ।।

anyatra dharmād anytrādharmād
anyatrāsmāt kr̥tākr̥tāt ।
anyatra bhūtāc ca bhavyāc ca
yat tat paśyasi tad vada ॥ 14 ॥

(Naciketas said:) What you perceive as apart from righteousness and apart from non-righteousness, apart from both effect and cause, apart from what has been and what is to be — tell me of 'that'.

Naciketas's competence to enter the mansion of eternal Happiness has been admitted by Yama, and now he (Naciketas) expresses his eagerness to enter. He does not know the inside of the house but Yama does, and therefore Naciketas asks to be led inside.

However, Naciketas does have some prescience of what he is about to see: It would be something beyond the duality of *dharma* and *adharma*, *kr̥ta* and *akr̥ta*, *bhūta* and *bhavya*.

Dharma as a social concept means moral virtue and righteousness and is to be practised in life by strictly adhering to scriptural injunctions. *Dharma*, derived from the root *dhr̥*, to support, means that which sustains and supports. In the philosophical context, it signifies the overall functional system of the world, maintaining its functional unity in spite of all the unpredictable vagaries of events. To recognize it as the leading force of life and to adhere to it in all practical matters is the *dharma* to be observed by man. To lead one's life without consideration for the all-sustaining system and other beings which are part of it, is *adharma* (unrighteous). The philosophical concept of *dharma* has no opposite in the word *adharma*, whilst as a social norm it is not so. To do anything forbidden is *adharma*; not to do something enjoined in scriptures is also *adharma*. The abode of eternal Happiness Naciketas is about to enter, he knows, is not bound by any such obligations. It is the Substance from which emanate all such dual concepts.

Kr̥ta means that which is done, that which is effected; *akr̥ta*, its opposite, is that which is not yet effected, that which still remains potential in the cause. What we call cause and effect are nothing more than different stages which are perceived by the human mind in the otherwise beginningless and endless transformation of nature, called 'becoming' in philosophical jargon. The Substance that undergoes this transformation or becoming is Being, the Reality Naciketas is about to behold, and it is beyond the duality of cause and effect, *akṛta* and *kṛta*.

The gold in a gold-chain, before its assuming the present form, must have been existing in some other form. Those past forms of the gold pertain to the *bhūta*, what has been. The same gold will, likewise, change its present form and will continue to exist in some new form, all possibilities hidden in the future, called *bhavya*. Likewise is the Reality Naciketas is about to behold. It had been assuming the form of everything in this world that had emerged and disappeared in the past (*bhūta*); it will assume all the forms yet to emerge in future in the world, as the world. Yet it will remain the same, unchanged.

सर्वे वेदा यत्पदमामनन्ति
तपांसि सर्वाणि च यद्वदन्ति ।
यदिच्छन्तो ब्रह्मचर्यं चरन्ति
तत् ते पदं सङ्ग्रहेण ब्रवीम्योमित्येतत् ।। १५ ।।

sarve vedā yat padam āmananti
tapāṁsi sarvāṇi ca yad vadanti ।
yad icchanto brahmacaryaṁ caranti
tat te padaṁ saṁgrahena bravīmi om ity
etat ।। 15 ।।

(Yama said:) The Word which all the Vedas declare, which all the austere enquiries proclaim (as goal), aimed at which *brahmacarya* is practised in life — that Word I shall tell you put in a nutshell: It is *AUṀ*.

AUṀ iti etat (It is *AUṀ*), the concluding words of this stanza, the sum and substance of the teaching any wisdom teacher has to impart to any disciple, constitute the whole of the interior of the mansion Naciketas was anxiously waiting to see; the rest of the Upanisad merely an elaboration. How the entire range of reality, from the most subtle to the most gross, subjective as well as objective, is signified by this monosyllable is the theme of meditation of the *Māṇḍūkya Upaniṣad*. A detailed study of it, along with the *kārikā* (versified comments) by Gauḍapāda is recommended here.

The wisdom represented by *AUṀ* is what all the scriptures of the world intend to convey in different ways; it is the goal aimed at by those who undergo austere practices and an ascetic life; it is the sole aim of those who transform their very life into a path in search of the Absolute (*Brahman*), known as *brahmacārins*.

The Upaniṣads, though of Indian origin, teach universal Truth. At the time when they were composed, possibly, none of the other civilizations of the world or religions were known to the *ṛṣis*, and hence they had in mind, when they used the word *veda*s, only the four Vedas of India. But we, of the present age, have to understand the word as denoting all the scriptures, as the word *veda* originally means. Scriptures, irrespective of their religious grounding, try to reveal the Absolute, each in its own way. An unprejudiced attempt to understand how the Absolute is conceived in each religion with the peculiarities of the historical and cultural background of its origin, would help to a great extent to save mankind from current religious feuds.

Realizable only as the essence of one's own being, the Absolute is not a knowable object. Interiorizing one's search by reversing the enquiring mind by 180° from its familiar direction of objective enquiry, is the only way to attain this subjective realization. Such a self-enquiry, rather unusual, needs the unrelenting self-heating on *tapas* which in effect envelops the whole being of the person concerned. All masters have passed through such a stage in life, often suffering even physical mortification. No seeker can attain it without undergoing the very same self-discipline. The *Bhagavad Gītā*, discribes it as a rather gentle process, and categorizes it as physical, mental and verbal (XVII.14-16). All such self-disciplines, austerities and asceticism, have only one final goal in view: the wisdom contained in *AUṀ*.

Upon its realization, one will live only in full harmony with It; as a manifest form of It; such a way of living is called *brahmacarya*, *carya* meaning walking about or way of life. One who is in search of Reality leads his life along a path conducive to his goal, which way of living is also *brahmacarya*. Students normally would be unmarried, and those who have attained the goal would have a natural disposition not to get involved in worldly affairs for their own sake, to the extent that they forgo all aspects of the worldly life including marriage; which is why they happen to be celebates. Abstinence from sex thus became implied in the meaning of the word *brahmacarya*, though the word does not mean it.

The Indian concept of human life considers that it has to pass through four stages, the first being *brahmacarya* or studenthood; the others are *gārhastya* (householder), *vānaprastha* (to be a self-negating forest-dweller mostly along with wife) and *saṁnyāsa* (final renunciation). This way of ordering one's life-span could also be considered as inspired by an intuitive vision of the meaning content of *AUṀ*.

एतद्ध्येवाक्षरं ब्रह्म एतद्ध्येवाक्षरं परम् ।
एतद्ध्येवाक्षरं ज्ञात्वा यो यदिच्छति तस्य तत् ।। १६ ।।

etaddhyevākṣaraṁ brahma etad dhyevākṣaraṁ
param ।
etaddhyevākṣaraṁ jñātvā yo yad icchati
tasya tat ।। 16 ।।

This (Imperishable) syllable is *Brahman;*
The (Imperishable) syllable is the Transcendental;
Knowing this (Imperishable) syllable,
Whatever one desires will indeed be his.

Now begins a series of meditations on the esoteric meaning content of the syllable *AUṀ*.

Any letter of the alphabet is called *akṣara* in the Sanskrit language; letters and syllables being the same in that language, a syllable is also known as *akṣara,* though literally it means 'the imperishable', the opposite of *kṣara* (the perishable). The word *akṣara*, as is used here, signifies both senses: the syllable *AUṀ* as well as the imperishable Reality signified by it. The Reality is none other than *Brahman*, the Absolute. Derived from the root *bṛh*, meaning 'to grow', the word *Brahman* means that which is endlessly growing. Manifest forms emerge from It beginninglessly and endlessly. Beyond all dimensions in magnitude, It is without beginning and end. It grows beyond any conceivable magnitude; so It is *Brahman*. It is the one eternal, invisible Reality underlying all that is visible and transient (*kṣara*).

Everything visible being transient, the eternal Reality is beyond everything visible and thus it is the transcendental (*param*).

Knowing this Imperishable Reality is, in essence, the seeker's realizing his own substance, even as a wave realizes itself as water in essence. To know it means to forgo one's identity with visible forms and conditioning factors, and identifying oneself with one Reality. Finding this identity with the Real, one discovers that the will and desire of the Real, the will and desire of nature, and one's own will and desire are the same. Having nothing more desirable than the Absolute to attain, its attainment in principle is the attainment of all desires.

एतदालम्बनं श्रेष्ठमेतदालम्बनं परम् ।
एतदालम्बनं ज्ञात्वा ब्रह्मलोके महीयते ।। १७ ।।

etad ālambanaṁ śreṣṭham etad ālambanaṁ param ।
etad ālambanaṁ jñātvā brahmaloke mahīyate ।। 17 ।।

It is the best of all abodes,
It is the transcendental abode;
Knowing it as the abode,
One attains greatness in the world of *Brahman*.

Life is so structured that the existence of everything necessarily depends on something else; everything together forming a structurally and functionally coherent whole. Certain things are more dependant than others; certain things are to be more depended on than others. The human mind has conceived the idea of superiority and inferiority by virtue of permanency, dependability and advantageousness. Even when everything considered dependable fails, there is one basic support that never fails; one abode is always there to accept and accommodate us, and to give us solace: *Brahman,* the Reality signified by *AUṀ*, called God in religious terms. Itself boundless, no one ever remains outside Its bounds. It is the never failing abode, the never failing refuge.

To depend on the Absolute is unlike the dependence on something else. It in effect is to depend on oneself, to depend on the Self, which is no dependence at all. Depending on something else is conditional whilst depending on oneself is unconditional, analogous to the dependence of an ornament on gold. The Absolute, the abode of everything therefore is considered the incomparably best abode (*śreṣtha*), an abode dependant on which one transcends even dependance, and thus a *param* (transcendental) abode.

Self-dependence attains its finality when it becomes the independence of the Absolute. The world is called *loka* in Sanskrit, literally that which could be looked at. Realizing the underlying substance in oneself means realizing the Substance underlying the whole world; knowing oneself means knowing all; depending on oneself means depending on the whole world and depending on the reality underlying the whole world. He who has attained this knowledge finds himself one with the world, one with the Real; finds himself in the world of *Brhaman* (*brahma-loka*), the whole world being the manifest form of *Brahman*. Such a person is loved by all, honoured by all, as his love for himself extends to all. The word *mahīyate* (attains greatness) implies adorability also. The most adorable being *Brahman*, he who finds himself one with *Brahman* is also equally adorable.

न जायते म्रियते वा विपश्चि-
नायं कुतश्चिन्न बभूव कश्चित् ।
अजो नित्यः शाश्वतोऽयं पुराणो
न हन्यते हन्यमाने शरीरे ।। १८ ।।

na jāyate mriyate vā vipaścin-
nāyaṁ kutaścin na babhūva kaścit ।
ajo nityaḥ śāśvato'yaṁ purāṇo
na hanyate hanyamāne śarīre ।। 18 ।।

The all-knowing one (the Self) is never born nor does it die. Not originating from anywhere, nothing originates from It. Unborn, everlasting, eternal, the most ancient. It is not destroyed on the destruction of the body (*śarīra*).

One of the key verses of this Upaniṣad, repeated almost verbatim in the *Bhagavad Gītā* (II.20), this stanza summarizes the Vedāntic notion of *Brahman*. Directly related to the question asked by Naciketas, it propounds concisely how life is visualized by the Upaniṣads, the problem of death and after-death not excluded. All elaborations that follow have therefore to be understood in the light of this verse. Or else, the students may be side-tracked by prevailing popular notions such as that of rebirth. Reality does not die; what does seemingly die then is not the real. The question asked therefore has bearings on the unreal. It vanishes on knowing the Real, the birthless and deathless.

Along with the problem of death goes the problem of birth. Along with the problem of hereafter goes the problem of here-now. Both are to be seen, as the Upaniṣads envision, as pertaining to the cosmic system of existence and life. Total existence is analogous to the ocean and has in it countless waves constantly arising and remerging; each individual is a wave in the ocean of Being. The emergence of a wave is what we call birth; its merging back into the ocean is death. Nothing is born, nothing is destroyed; what always was, is and will be, is the ocean of Being alone. An individual wave on knowing itself, finds itself one with the birthless and deathless ocean, thus itself immortal. Such a wise one is called *vipaścit*.

Any knowledge, in essence, is nothing but a wave formulation in the ocean of consciousness which is the total Reality. Reality is pure unconditioned consciousness and is always conscious of everything that gets formulated in its Being, and is also *vipaścit*, the Wise One. The knower of Reality being one with *Brahman*, whatever could be said of *Brahman* could be said of him too. It is this immortal Reality that is signified by *AUṀ*.

The Vedāntic perspective of Reality, metaphysically is known as *sat-kāraṇa-vāda*, the theory that cause alone is real, effect having no existence of its own. The world and all the evanescent appearances in it are all effects having no existence apart from that of the causal Reality, *sat*, *Brahman*. All appearances are changeful, the causal Reality changeless. The world in this sense is often called *jagat* (that which always goes on).

That the Reality we are in search of is not an effect is implied in the words, 'Not originated from anywhere', and that neither is It a cause of anything is implicit in, 'Nothing originated from It'. Itself neither cause nor effect, Reality as unfolding itself as everything, is thought of by the enquiring mind as the cause of all appearances. Given that the emergence and existence of effect has no reality apart from that of the causal Reality, causality as such also becomes meaningless. Cause-effect relationship is but an idea projected by the human mind onto the incessant flow of events appearing in Self-Reality, in order to make the continuity of the flow reasonably comprehensible.

Accustomed to system units and their sciences, the human mind in any of its pursuits perfers to systematize what is being studied, to relate the component factors of a system in terms of cause and effect. Failing to systematize, one feels what is being studied is a mystery. Causality, in short, is not an experienced natural phenomenon; it is simply an attribute ascribed to the continuity of the natural flow of events; and thus the duality of cause and effect, a human concept, is not a natural fact. The *sat-kāraṇa-vāda* (the theory that cause alone is real) is also therefore valid in the field of conceptualization, of isms. Intuitive perception being all that matters in the final certitude of Reality, one finds oneself, on its attainment, beyond the duality of cause and effect. One of this attainment is to be called *vipaścit* (a wise one).

Destruction of an ornament-form does not mean the destruction of gold. So too, the destruction of individual beings does not imply the destruction of the Reality underlying them. Such visible, destructible aspect of any being is called *śarīra*, meaning, the destructible, in Sanskrit. The *Bhagavad Gītā*, defining *śarīra* (XIII.5,6), brings under it all that is perishable in an individual being, from the grossest physical factors up to and including the animating principle (*cetanā*), what in religious terms is called 'soul'. What endures even on the destruction of all such individuating factors is the Reality signified by *AUṀ*, the Reality that underlies all those individuating factors.

हन्ता चेन्मन्यते हन्तुं हतश्चेन्मन्यते हतम् ।
उभौ तौ न विजानीतो नायं हन्ति न हन्यते ।। १९ ।।

hantā cen manyate hantuṁ hataś cen manyate
hatam ।
ubhau tau na vijānīto nāyaṁ hanti na hanyate ।। 19 ।।

If the slayer thinks of slaying,
If the slain thinks himself slain,
Both these understand not;
This one slays not, nor is it slain.

Happening to kill some being, one thinks of himself as a killer. The act of killing destroys only the visible individuating factors in the other being, not the indestructible Reality-content of it. He is not the killer of

Reality. So too, one who is being killed thinks he is being killed, whilst the Reality in him endures undestroyed. The Reality is never killed. It never kills; only apparent forms of It get changed. The slayer thinks of himself as a slayer as he identifies himself with the *śarīra,* as he identifies the being of the dead one as its *śarīra.* So too the killed, thinking himself slain, identifies himself with his *śarīra*. Each forgets the one underlying Reality in oneself.

Birth and death, killing and being killed, are all events incessantly occurring everywhere in nature. A distinct unit this flow of events, separated out and seen at its varying stages of progression, is considered as having in it cause and effect, a preceding stage of events considered cause and the succeeding stage effect. Each individual being is an inseparable part of this incessant flow of nature's self-unfoldment, every stage of which involving an activity or *karma*. Human beings involved in such *karmas* are, due to ignorance, filled with the wrong notion that they personally are the doers of those actions. The real doer is nature alone. Knowing that one is merely instrumental in all actions and that all actions, including our willing freely, take place actually in the totality of nature or one Reality, one becomes unattached to all actions and thus frees oneself from the bondages caused by them. All actions being of nature, an individual has no action (*karma*) of his own, nor is he the doer of actions (*kartā*). This understanding absolves one of all sins in life.

A problem then arises: Is it all right to kill someone on the claim that the act of killing was done by nature? The wise one sees all his acts as pertaining to nature as part of his seeing himself also an inseparable part of nature. His love for himself, the most fundamental love one has, as a natural corollary, widens and becomes the love for all. Not willing to kill himself, he will not desire to kill another being, as he sees himself in every being. He would not have any desire of his own except of doing what is natural to him as an individual, as part of the whole. Whatever occurs in such a course of life, not willed by him, whether in the form of helping others or hurting others, would not be considered his own acts. Those who think they are the doers of actions become worried whether those actions were right or wrong, whether meritorious or sinful. Once freed of the sense of agency of actions, one becomes free of both sin and merit. Life is part of the self-unfoldment of nature, so too are actions. A wise one, with no sense of agency of actions (*kartṛtva*), lives as part of nature, doing whatever the chance element of nature demands, with no sense of sin or merit, with no desire to do anything on his own. A sense of responsibility, value sense, all these being part of nature in man, he has to make use of them properly to live as part of nature, as a person responsible to nature, not to any particular individual, group or community. Once endowed with this higher sense of responsibility, one will never tend to think of making use of a basic principle of life an excuse for killing a fellow being.

Also repeated almost verbatim in the *Bhagavad Gītā* (II.19), this verse puts emphasis on the metaphysical aspect of the immortality of Reality, whilst in the *Gītā*, the moral aspect, the eradication of confoundedness Arjuna was in, concerning the sinfulness of the impending and inevitable killing of his own kith and kin, was also of concern.

अणोरणीयान् महतो महीया-
नात्मास्य जन्तोर्निहितो गुहायाम् ।
तमक्रतुः पश्यति वीतशोको
धातुप्रसादान्महिमानमात्मनः ।। २० ।।

aṇor aṇīyān mahato mahīyān
ātmāsya jantor nihito guhāyām ।
tam akratuḥ paśyati vītaśoko
dhātuprasādān mahimānam ātmanaḥ ।। 20 ।।

Minuter than the minutest, greater than the greatest, the Self (*ātman*) abides hidingly in all beings. One without active will, freed from sorrow, beholds the glory of the Self, by the grace of the all-sustaining One.

The Reality symbolized by *AUM*, portrayed in Stanzas 16 through 19, and now presented as *ātman* (the Self), is full of contradictions when logically viewed as is being shown from this stanza onwards. Nevertheless, it is not unattainable. It reveals itself to the one who surrenders himself, along with all his active willing for activities motivated by personal gains, to that Reality. The desires of the one who always finds himself one with the one Reality, will also be naturally one with those of the Reality. The word *akratu*, rendered here as 'the one without active will' also means 'not interested in ritual', *kratu* then meaning ritualistic sacrifice.

One's effort alone is enough to get an intellectual understanding of anything, but the revelation of the Reality is a two-way process: intuitive self-enquiry on the part of the seeker blessed by the all-sustaining One, understood either as *ātman* (the Self) or *Īśvara* (God).

Ātman (the Self), now introduced in this Upaniṣad, is 'the Imperishable' of Verse 16, the 'best abode' of Verse 17, the 'birthless and deathless Substance' of Verse 18, the 'one who neither kills nor is killed' of Verse 19, and is not simply the soul or animating principle as is usually conceived. It is the one Substance that pervades (*ātatam*) all apparent forms (*śarīra),* even as gold pervades all the apparent forms of ornaments, as its etymological root *āt* means (*āt vyāpane*, the root *āt* in the sense 'to pervade'). *Śarīra*, loosely translated as 'body', strictly speaking means 'the destructible', which includes within its ambit the physical aspect of existence at one extreme and the animating principle at the other and all that comes in between, as the *Bhagavad Gītā* makes clear, which we have already noticed under Verse 18 above. The Substance that assumes this entire range of appearances is the *ātman* and thus it is the all-sustaining One (*dhātā*) of this verse.

Appearance alone being measurable, the substance that underlies it remains always unmeasured and immeasurable. *Ātman*, appearing as the subtlest and minutest aspect of existence as well as the most expansive and gross, in itself is neither minute nor expansive, or else, it is minuter than the minutest and greater than the greatest.

The Substance, not being an object of knowledge, is to be perceived intuitively (*paśyati*). Philosophy itself is called *darśana* in Sanskrit, which also means intuitive perception. It is visualizing oneself as the Substance one appears as, even as an ornament visualizes itself as gold.

All sorrows are personal, whereas every person is an inseparable part of the total Existence. Events become cause of sufferings for man as he sees himself as separate from the whole, and separate from others. The final solution for all sufferings is seeing oneself one with the whole.

The desire to know Reality does not arise in all; proper guidance in the search may not be obtainable to those who are desirous of it. Their coincidence occurs in life only by chance, as though by the grace of God, the all sustaining One (*dhātā*). The word *dhātuprasāda* is interpretable in two ways: as the grace of *dhātā* (the all-sustainer) and as the grace *dhātus* (the basic physical elements of body), seven in number according to the ancient Indian medical science: *rasa* (fluids), *rakta* (blood), *māṁsa* (flesh), *medas* (fat), *asthi* (bones), *majjā* (marrow), and *śukla* (semen). A healthy body with a healthy combination of all these elements along with a healthy mind, is essential for the sustained effort absolutely necessary in any search for Reality.

आसीनो दूरं व्रजति शयानो याति सर्वतः ।
कस्तं मदामदं देवं मदन्यो ज्ञातुमर्हति ।। २१ ।।

āsīno dūraṁ vrajati śayāno yāti sarvataḥ ।
kas taṁ madāmadaṁ devaṁ madanyo
jñātumarhati ।। 21 ।।

Sitting still, It moves afar;
Lying down, It goes everywhere;
Who, save myself, is able to know
that effulgent Being who rejoices
and rejoices not?

Elaborating on what appear as paradoxes, when logically viewed, this verse says, remaining still It reaches out everywhere. The Self as *sat* (Existence) is experienced by each of us as our own self-existence; but It exists everywhere as everything. As *cit* (consciousness) It, is conscious of everything everywhere. It is faster than light getting to its objects. Pure Consciousness, It is also *deva*, the Effulgent Being.

Ānanda (Happiness) in essence, Its absolute form is *mada* (rejoicing); and relatively It appears as the pleasures and pains of actual life (*mada* and *amada*). Yet It remains non-dual, unaffected by such conceptual differentiations.

The Self is to be known as oneself, by oneself, for oneself. Yama's knowledge of the Self is as himself, by himself, for himself. Naciketas has to know the Self in this same way, for himself. Every logical knowledge is of an object by a subject; Self-knowledge is an objectless, subjectless, Self-awareness.

अशरीरं शरीरेष्वनवस्थेष्ववस्थितम् ।
महान्तं विभुमात्मानं मत्वा धीरो न शोचति ।। २२ ।।

aśarīraṁ śarīreṣvanavastheṣvavasthitam ।
mahāntaṁ vibhum ātmānaṁ matvā dhīro
na śocati ।। 22 ।।

Existing firm, as the bodiless in and through all the bodies, the stable abiding in and through all that is unstable, the great, the all-pervading is the *ātman*. Knowing It the wise one laments not in life.

To know what steel is one has only to examine closely something such as a nail-clipper made of steel, as the *Chāndogya Upaniṣad* explains. The form of the nail-clipper is the body aspect (*śarīra*) assumed by its *ātman*, steel. All assumed forms are alterable at will; the steel content is unalterable. Likewise, to know the Self, the one Substance in all worldly appearances, one has only to examine the essential content of oneself. One's body — aggregate of all the individuating factors, from the physical body to the animating principle — is born, it grows and disappears at death, but its self-content remains unalterable, eternal. Yet the eternal cannot and will not exist without assuming some changeful form, the world, as eternal steel cannot exist except in some form or another, always transient. The eternal, invisible Reality thus exists in and through evanescent, visible forms called the world. It is the all-pervading Reality (*vibhu*) in all that is visible (*loka*), the world.

The changeful *śarīra* aspect of existence is often classified as *sthūla śarīra* (gross body) consisting of the aggregate of physical elements, *sūkṣma śarīra* (subtle body) the aggregate of subtle aspects such as sense and mind, and *kāraṇa śarīra* (causal body), the unconsciously functioning animating principle. The Reality that pervades all these apparent individuating factors, not perceivable as such, is the great (*mahat*) which word also means the worshippable. God (*Īśvara*), the most worshippable understood by all religions, is none other than this Self-Reality in the capacity of the all-pervading (*vibhu*). Knowing the unborn, indestructible Self as one's essential content, forgoing one's identity with the evanescent apparent form (*śarīra*), one finds oneself immortal, and thus devoid of all fears and afflictions caused by the thought of death. One finds one's own beingness stabilized in the Self and thus becomes *dhīra*, which word means one who is firm as well as one who knows Reality and imparts that knowledge to others.

नायमात्मा प्रवचनेन लभ्यो
न मेधया न बहुना श्रुतेन ।
यमेवैष वृणुते तेन लभ्य-
स्तस्यैष आत्मा विवृणुते तनूं स्वाम् ।। २३ ।।

nāyam ātmā pravacanena labhyo
na medhayā na bahunā śrutena ।
yam evaiṣa vṛṇute tena labhyaḥ
tasyaiṣa ātmā vivṛṇute tanūṁ svām ।। 23 ।।

This Self is unattainable by instruction, by intellectual power, nor even through much learning of scriptures.
It is attainable to one It chooses;
To such a person It reveals Itself wholly.

Symbolized by *AUṀ*, the Self is the Reality underlying everything in this phenomenal world, the *śarīra* referred to in the last verse. The phenomenal world consists not merely of perceptible objects, but includes the perceiving mind also. Narayana Guru, one of the *ṛṣis* of this century, defined the phenomenal world as 'the aggregate of thousands of names, thousands of concepts and thousands of corresponding objects' (*Advaita Deepika*,Verse 1). To learn, be it about the Abosolute, is a function of mind; so too are thinking and formulating ideas and images. Yet the Substance that manifests as the thinking mind, never becomes an object conceivable by the mind, just as eye never becomes its own object of vision.

To claim that the Absolute is unattainable either by instruction or by thinking might seem too tall a claim and even apparently contradicting some other Upaniṣadic teachings. The *Taittirī ya Upaniṣad*, for example, enjoins,'One should not be negligent of study and instruction' (I.11.1). Śaṅkara, in his *Vivekacūḍāmaṇi*, also claims,'one who is learned, intelligent and proficient in intuitive knowledge' alone is competent to Self-knowledge. All thinking, all learning, all listening to discourses (*pravacana*) helps only get clear the way for the enquiry; they never take the seeker to the final attainment.

This goal is attained, the text claims, only as a result of the Self's choosing the seeker. An individual, every seeker is a form chosen by the Self and assumed by the Self for its own self-manifestation. It is to the one who feels of himself that he is an apparent form of the Self, endowed with the quest for the Self, that the Self reveals itself in its full glory, like a wife reveals her whole being before her chosen husband.

Naciketas chose the Self — the secret behind birth and death — as his third boon: the Self chose Naciketas to reveal Itself to. Who chose whom is a delicate question, better left unanswered.

It is not as if no thinking, learning, reading of scriptures is needed for the attainment of this goal. The Self and the seeker having mutually chosen, the seeker, assisted by learning, thinking and instruction, attains the final goal.

नाविरतो दुश्चरितान्नाशान्तो नासमाहितः ।
नाशान्तमानसो वापि प्रज्ञानेनैनमाप्नुयात् ।। २४ ।।

nāvirato duścaritān nāśānto nāsamāhitaḥ ।
nāśānta-mānaso vāpi prajñānenainam
āpnuyāt ।। 24 ।।

Unless desisting from evil conducts, unless tranquil, unless composed, unless of peaceful mind, one attains It not through intelligence alone.

The Self's choosing the seeker, a favourable factor in the attainment of Self-knowledge, was emphasized in the last verse; the present verse puts stress on the need for the seeker to be resolute, unrelenting and full of self-restraint. Instead of subjecting oneself to a self-imposed discipline, self-restraint has to become spontaneous in the day-to-day life of the seeker. Not related as cause and effect, this self-restraint and the accomplishment aimed at make each other meanigful, one meaningless without the other. For the one still a seeker, this self-restraint is a means of accomplishment; for one of accomplished goal it is his way of life.

To desist from evil deeds has always been considered a moral responsibility of man, yet fixing a criterion to decide which is good and which is bad has always evaded all philosophizing. Narayana Guru, for the first time in the history of philosophy, addressed himself to this problem and said: Deeds fully in agreement with the oneness of the Self are good; acts which bring happiness to oneself and others together are good. Deeds which violate the oneness of the Self are evil; acts which result in one's own happiness and in the unhappiness of others are evil. Seekers as well as knowers of the Self cannot therefore turn a deaf ear towards moral demands.

Deliberate committing of evil deeds is to be distinguished from those committed owing to ignorance; the former incorrigible and the latter corrigible. The ignorant, with no desire to know reality and to desist from evil, are also not rescuable; Self-knowledge will always remain unaccomplished for them.

Slipping into error, tempted by the mind and senses, is a common occurrence even among those who clearly discriminate good and evil. Mind thinking of the possibility of pleasure tempts the senses to be active in relating to objects which actualize those pleasures; conversely, incidentally perceiving something attractive tempts mind to fancy the pleasure derivable from it. Inadvertent deflecting from one's chosen path is thus possible both ways.

The mind, when awake, is always in need of and is in search of something to be interested in; it refuses to be inactive. To make mind inactive, even as a spiritual discipline, would in effect be equivalent to starving it. The healthiest spiritual discipline would therefore be to show the mind the best object to be interested in, the master-interest in life — the self-contentment of Self-awareness in the present case. As the mind gets interested in the lasting and the highest of all values it spontaneously desists from interesting itself in those of less and flickering value. This spontaneous self-withdrawal could be made more effective and fruitful by self-restraint as a spiritual discipline. Restraining the mind and senses and making the mind directed to the master interest have thus to go hand in hand, one making the other more effective.

The *Bhagavad Gītā,* whenever it dwells on this aspect, does not loose sight of this two-faced nature of systematic Self-enquiry. For example, Chapter II says (Verse 59):

The sense-objects turn away from him
who does not feed upon them, but the
taste for them persists. On seeing the
Supreme even this taste ceases.

यस्य ब्रह्म च क्षत्रं च उभे भवत ओदनः ।
मृत्युर्यस्योपसेचनं क इत्था वेद यत्र सः ।। २५ ।।

yasya brahma ca kṣatraṁ ca ubhe bhavata odanaḥ ।
mṛtyur yasyopasecanaṁ ka itthā veda
yatra saḥ ।। 25 ।।

Yearning to know (*brahma*) and aptitude for activity (*kṣatra*), both are staple food for It, and death Its sauce. Who knows where It is?

A new-born child needs nourishment for its growth and sustenance, and this need lasts till the last moment of life. The nourishing food should be tasty too. Every being that emerges, the Vedāntin considers, is a specific form in which the one Self finds self-expression owing to the invincible creative urge inherent in It. The Self, aware of what becomes of It, has *Brahman*-hood (the all inclusive consciousness aspect) implicit in It; ever creative, it has *kṣatra*-hood (activeness) implicit in It; both serving as nourishing factors in the ever new becoming of ever new forms. The emergence of new forms, called birth, implies the disappearance of old forms, which we call death, as the emergence of a chick implies the disappearance of the egg. Birth and death together thus makes the nourishing food of life tastier, keeping it ever new.

The *Brahman* and *kṣatra* characteristics implicit in the Self, as they become explicit as human characteristics in the phenomenal world, appear as the brāhmaṇa-hood and kṣatriya-hood of man, both conducive to Self-knowledge, when aware of. Being the only Reality and Its own nourishing factor, how can one say where the Self is? Whatever could be considered as Its abode, had emerged from It and was nourished by It.

Naciketas's desire to know that which is neither *dharma* nor *adharma*, neither cause nor effect, neither of the past nor of the future, was satisfied by Yama's reply from Verses 15 to 25. How *AUṀ* symbolizes this non-dual Reality which is nothing but *ātman* and how It is to be known were also summarily explained. The concluding Verse of this chapter opens the doorway to the next chapter wherein will be shown how every individual entity in this world is a specific form of unfoldment of *AUṀ*, the one Reality, the Self.

Chapter III

तृतीया वल्ली

ऋतं पिबन्तौ सुकृतस्य लोके
गुहां प्रविष्टौ परमे परार्धे ।
छायातपौ ब्रह्मविदो वदन्ति
पञ्चाग्नयो ये च त्रिणाचिकेताः ।। १ ।।

ṛtaṁ pibantau sukṛtasya loke
guhāṁ praviṣṭau parame parārdhe ।
chāyātapau brahmavido vadanti
pañcāgnayo ye ca triṇāciketāḥ ।। 1 ।।

Two relishers of the results of actions are there in the world of properly performed actions, and they dwell in the secret abode in the highest upper sphere. Knowers of *Brahman* speak of them as 'light' and 'shadow' and so do house-holders who maintain the five sacrificial fires, and those too who perform the triple Nāciketa fire.

THE transitory stage from Vedic ritualism to Vedāntic wisdom is the milieu in which the teaching of this Upaniṣad is set, indicated by the ritual performed by Vājaśravasa and also by the second and third boons chosen by Naciketas. So too is Yama's christening by Naciketas's name the fire-sacrifice instructed to Naciketas. Appropriate to such a setting, the words *ṛta* and *sukṛta* are interpretable both as belonging to ritual and to wisdom.

Sukṛtam in the context of ritual means the rites well performed as enjoined by the Vedas; *ṛtam* is the result of the ritual enjoyed by men.

It, in the wisdom content, is the well-done (*su*) actions (*kṛta*) of the Self. Whatever appears as existent in the world and as the world is a self-manifestation of the Self-Reality, and is effected by the invincible creative urge (*karma*) inherent in It. No self-expression goes wrong. The self-expression of the Self therefore has to be an action well-done (*sukṛta*). It has in it an invincible system of its own beginningless and endless events, each event resulting in another event. This functional system, along with the result of each event, is called *ṛtam*. The Self itself is the enjoyer of such results; man, as an enjoyer, is only a manifested aspect of It. Everything that occurs as a part of the course of events in nature is *sukṛta* (properly performed deed), and every result occurring is *ṛtam*, the Self itself its enjoyer. This *sukṛta* concept is well displayed in the *Taittirīya Upaniṣad* when it says:

> This world in the beginning verily was non-existent. Therefrom indeed was the existent born. It (*Brahman*) created itself by itself. Therefore it is called well-made (*sukṛta*). (II.7.1)

The Self, existing everywhere, has no particular abode of Its own and thus, It is as though hiding secretly. Thinking of the Self as dwelling in a cave-like secret place — often misinterpreted as heart — thus became a prevailing idea in Vedānta. This secret abode is understood to be in the highest region (*parame*) and is in the upper sphere (*parārdhe*). It is so inconceivable and unimaginable that It dwells in a region highest in the physical sense. *Parārdha*, a word of multiple connotations, means the other part, the latter half; it also is the highest countable number according to ancient Indian mathematicians, a number in which 1 is followed by 17 zeroes. All these are suggestive of the other side of the conceivable and quantifiable aspects of the world. It is thus not a region spatially high above everything; its highness is in its subtlity and sublimity.

Though not clarified in the text, who the two enjoyers are will become clear in the course of this chapter. The one relishes the Freedom of life with full sense of detachment and self-restraint; the other gets involved in everything giving pleasure and enjoys them; both possibilities exist in the Self, like light and shadow. These enjoyers are quite similar to the two birds portrayed in the *Muṇḍaka Upaniṣad* (III.i.1) and *Śvetāśvatara Upaniṣad* (IV.6), one eating berries and the other just watching.

Such a classification of enjoyment is acceptable to both the knowers of *Brahman* and to ritualists, though in different senses. The latter considers that those who perform ritual and meritorious deeds, enjoy the light side, and that those who do not care for them and do evil deeds enjoy the shadow side. The 'light' side, according to *Brahman*-knowers and seekers is the supreme joy of Self-realization, enjoyable only with full restraint of the mind and senses, and the 'shadow' side the pleasures enjoyed by unrestrained minds. The Nāciketa fire, the fire represented by Naciketas, taught by Yama, serves as a bridge between the value worlds of ritualism and wisdom as will be made explicit in the next verse and as suggested in the present one.

यः सेतुरीजानानामक्षरं ब्रह्म यत् परम् ।
अभयं तितीर्षतां पारं नाचिकेतं शकेमहि ।। २ ।।

yaḥ setur ījānānām akṣaraṁ brahma yat param ।
abhayaṁ titīrṣatāṁ pāraṁ nāciketaṁ śakemahi ।। 2 ।।

The Nāciketa fire, the bridge for the sacrificers, the highest imperishable *Brahman* for those who seek to cross over to the fearless farther shore — may we master it.

The symbolic Nāciketa fire, the bridge between the way of ritual and the way of wisdom, belongs to neither of the paths and is beyond the two; it represents the real non-dual stance of the Upaniṣad. The adherents to both the paths are in search of self-happiness, a goal neither 'light' nor 'shade'. Any path is chosen at the dictates of the value sensing aspect (*ānanda*) of *Brahman*, aided by the thinking function of the Consciousness aspect (*cit*) of *Brahman*. *Brahman* — first introduced here in this Upaniṣad — thus provides for both the paths. Though beyond all logical reasoning, this imperishable Reality is not unattainable to knowledge. Oneself being that Reality in essence, one has only to become conscious of being That. Yama knows that Realilty as his own being; Naciketas too would know it to be as his own being. Yama therefore brackets them together and says, 'may we master it'.

This attainment is marked by fearlessness in life. One only fears the others or other things. One is not afraid of oneself. Seeing oneself in all beings, and all beings in oneself — the mark of attainment of Self-knowledge or *Brahman*-knowledge — one finds there is nothing to be scared of.

The world of birth and death is fraught with fear. Reaching the other shore of all phenomenal becoming, the other half (*parārdha*) of Reality, one finds oneself immortal and free of all fear of death, where the question of the hereafter also vanishes.

आत्मानं रथिनं विद्धि शरीरं रथमेव तु ।
बुद्धिं तु सारथिं विद्धि मनः प्रग्रहमेव च ।। ३ ।।

इन्द्रियाणि हयानाहुर्विषयांस्तेषु गोचरान् ।
आत्मेन्द्रियमनोयुक्तं भोक्तेत्याहुर्मनीषिणः ।। ४ ।।

ātmānaṁ rathinaṁ viddhi śarīraṁ ratham eva tu ।
buddhiṁ tu sārathiṁ viddhi manaḥ pragraham eva ca ।। 3 ।।

indriyāni hayān āhur viṣayāṁs teṣu gocarān ।
ātmendriya-mano-yuktaṁ bhoketyāhur manīṣiṇaḥ ।। 4 ।।

Know the self as the lord of the chariot, and body as the chariot. Know intellect as the charioteer, and mind as the rein.

Senses are said to be the horses, and sense-objects what they range over.

The Self, united with senses and mind, wise men say, is the enjoyer.

The imperishable *Brahman*, experienced by each one as the being of oneself, unfolds itself incessantly and multifariously as this world. The onward push for this unfoldment is what we call life, and each being feels this onward push as the search for new vistas of experiences; the more unexpected such experiences are the more they add to the novelty of life. It is this hope for novel experiences that makes life worth living, at least as far as man, the only being who thinks of the meaning of life, is concerned. The absence of such a push, a state of being when one is not interested in anything, is a fatal psychopathological condition, called *arati* in Sanskrit.

The unfailing interest of the Imperishable *Brahman* in unfolding Itself as this world, is in seeing for Itself what infinite potential is latent in Itself. As part of this self-unfoldment It assumes the form of all the bodies and uses them as the chariot, to ride on in search of new possibilities. A structural unit specifically devised for a particular purpose, the chariot is neither the wheels, the axle, the platform, the seat, the horses, the charioteer, nor any other of its component parts. It is a whole. All its component parts, as parts of a whole, are meant as aids in the one overall purpose: the search for self-happiness. *Śarīra*, the original Sanskrit word for body, means that which perishes. Compared to the chariot in the analogy, the body is not merely the seat of the senses, mind, intellect and so on, but is the aggregate of all these. It consists of everything perishable in a being, from gross physical elements upto and including the animating principle (*cetanā*), as the *Bhagavad Gītā* describes it, in Verses XIII.5, 6, all transient emanations from the one Imperishable Reality. United with such self-created conditionings, the Self, otherwise unconditioned, becomes the enjoyer (*bhoktā*). An individual in search of self-happiness as part of the self-unfoldment of *Brahman,* man's first concern should be on using these *Brahman*-given aids, for the realization of *Brahman*-reality in oneself and on seeing life's onward progress as the progression of the self-unfoldment of that Reality.

The chariot of the individuated self is the body; *Brahman*, the cosmic Self , rides the chariot of the cosmos. How *Brahman* rides the world-chariot is inconceivable to human mind, but man knows how he rides the body-chariot.

The destination of man's chariot-drive, when the meaning of life is properly understood, should be the attainment of fearlessness and immortality as indicated in the last verse. Master appoints a well-trained charioteer — here it is *buddhi*, the intellect — to help him reach the goal. The seeker therefore has to be vigilant in keeping the intellect sharp and attuned to the goal, lest the intellect should lead him astray, following its own whims.

The senses, constantly in quest of ever new objects of interest, constitute the main force that pulls life forward and thus they are like the horses of a chariot. It is through the senses that consciousness, the essence of the Self the master, finds expression. Unless goaded by the charioteer using of the rein, these horses are prone to be tempted by the tickling of momentary pleasures, for their own sake, forgetting what it is and why it has been devised by *Brahman*. The mind (*manas*), particularly its volition, is the bridle the charioteer (intellect) has to use masterfully. No intellectual understanding of the goal of life would be of any value unless associated with the will to stand by it.

The Self, by Itself unconditioned, when conditioned by Its identity with the body, senses, mind, intellect and so on, is known as the enjoyer (*bhoktā*). Every enjoyer enjoys objects other than himself. But the Self, when aware that the body, senses, intellect and all other conditioning factors are devised by Itself for Its own self-expression, and that they do not exist apart from Itself, finds Itself the enjoyer of Itself, and thus not an enjoyer in the ordinary sense of the word. Sheer Joy alone remains without the duality of enjoyer-enjoyed.

The same chariot analogy when adopted by Narayana Guru, the place of the body as chariot is taken by libido (*rati*), giving a psychological shift to the otherwise biological picture of the Upaniṣad. The Guru says:

> Yoked with horses such as hearing, and occupied by self's image, with the dextrous mental faculties for charioteer, the libido-chariot is mounted on by I-sense riding incessantly in search of peasurables external.
>
> (Verse 69, *Ātmopadeśa Śatakam*)

यस्त्वविज्ञानवान् भवत्ययुक्तेन मनसा सदा ।
तस्येन्द्रियाण्यवश्यानि दुष्टाश्वा इव सारथेः ।। ५ ।।

यस्तु विज्ञानवान् भवति युक्तेन मनसा सदा ।
तस्येन्द्रियाणि वश्यानि सदश्वा इव सारथेः ।। ६ ।।

yas tvavijñānavān bhavaty ayuktena manasā sadā ।
tasy endriyāṇyavaśyāni duṣṭāśvā iva sāratheḥ ।। 5 ।।

yastu vijñānavān bhavati yuktena manasā sadā ।
tasy endriyāṇi vaśyāni sadaśvā iva sāratheḥ ।। 6 ।।

With no understanding and mind not constantly held firm, one's senses go unrestrained like vicious horses to a charioteer. (5)

With understanding and mind constantly held firm, one's senses remain restrained, like good horses to a charioteer. (6)

With the chariot in good condition, the horses well trained, the charioteer discriminative, the horses well controlled, and all working in unison, the charioting expedition will be a success. What is basically helpful is an intellect capable of discriminating what the goal is and what distractions are present on the way. The original world *vijñāna*, rendered here as 'understanding', strictly means specific knowledge or applied knowledge. A seeker's *vijñāna* is in his ability to discriminating his life's goal, the realization of his own immortality. The *vijñāna* of a man of attainment consists in his seeing himself, everything in this world, as well as life itself, as a specific mode of expression of the one and only Reality, *Brahman*, thus seeing *Brahman* alone in everything, even in the actualities and day-to-day problems of life.

The mind being held firm unitively (*yukta*) implies non-dependence on external considerations in deciding what is to be done and to be gained in life, a quality known as *uparati* in Vedānta; the habit of relying only on the one all-sustaining Reality is known as *samādhāna*.

Forced restraint of the senses as a spiritual discipline would not help. Like good horses in the hands of an expert charioteer, the senses, instead of causing distraction, helps attain the goal.

यस्त्वविज्ञानवान् भवत्यमनस्कः सदाऽशुचिः ।
न स तत् पदमाप्नोति संसारं चाधिगच्छति ।। ७ ।।

यस्तु विज्ञानवान् भवति समनस्कः सदा शुचिः ।
स तु तत् पदमाप्नोति यस्माद् भूयो न जायते ।। ८ ।।

yas tvavijñānavān bhavati amanaskaḥ sadāśuciḥ ।
na sa tat padam āpnoti saṁsāraṁ
cādhigacchati ।। 7 ।।
yas tu vijñāṇavān bhavati samanaskaḥ sadā śuciḥ
sa tu tat padam āpnoti yasmād bhūyo na
jāyate ।। 8 ।।

One of no understanding, unmindful and always impure, reaches not the goal, but attains *saṁsāra*. (7)

One of understanding, mindful and always pure, reaches the goal, wherefrom he is born no more. (8)

The theme around which teaching develops in this Upaniṣad was portrayed in the first chapter. After showing how peculiar and exceptional was the nature of the Reality about to be made known to Naciketas, Yama leads him into the mansion of eternal Happiness, the Imperishable Self/*Brahman*, symbolized by *AUṀ*. Death is simply the flavouring element that makes *Brahman*'s Self-unfoldment enjoyable to Itself. The present chapter treats life as a charioting expedition of the Self with the apparent, perishable aspects of existence as the chariot and its accompaniments. The present two verses together depicts the possible failure or success of the expedition in reaching its destination.

The chariot in bad condition, ill-driven by an untrained charioteer, instead of reaching the destination of Immortality, leads to finding itself struggling in the ocean of becoming called *saṁsāra*. Denoting the worldly life of repetitions of birth and death, the word *saṁsāra* strictly means constant going on. Those who consider the changeful apparent forms of becoming as real see life as a cyclic process of birth and death in which everything is always changeful. But those who see the Self / *Brahman*, the 'Being' that undergoes this process of 'Becoming', as the Real, visualize It as birthless and deathless; identifying oneself with that Immortal Reality one finds oneself immortal — the final goal aimed at. One thus finds oneself on the farther shore of the ocean of *saṁsāra* or becoming, at the abode of ultimate Freedom (*mukti*), where the duality of birth and death, of joy and suffering, is unknown. In the absence of death, the question of the state after death becomes irrelevant.

विज्ञानसारथिर्यस्तु मनःप्रग्रहवान् नरः ।
सोऽध्वनः पारमाप्नोति तद् विष्णोः परमं पदम् ।। ९ ।।

vijñāna sārathir yas tu manaḥ-pragrahavān naraḥ ।
so'dhvanaḥ pāram āpnoti tad viṣṇoḥ paramaṁ padam ।। 9 ।।

With understanding for charioteer and well-utilized mind for reins, man reaches the destination of the journey, the Supreme abode of Viṣṇu.

The stanza introduces the idea of Viṣṇu whose abode is identified with the destination of life's journey. Viṣṇu, though understood popularly as the God of Sustenance, one of the three chief gods of the Hindu pantheon, in the present philosophical context means, that which is expansive. Though shown as the destination of life's journey, Viṣṇu, as the all-pervading Reality, is the substance that assumes the form of the track traversed as well, and thus is beyond the duality of ends and means.

Habitually we make efforts to know what consciousness is, whilst the very effort takes place in the same consciousness we are searching for. Consciousness, the essential substance of the Self/*Brahman*, is thus beyond the duality of ends and means, beyond the conditionings of time and space. Viṣṇu is the all-inclusive Reality, beyond all dualities.

इन्द्रियेभ्यः परा ह्यर्था अर्थेभ्यश्च परं मनः ।
मनसस्तु परा बुद्धिर्बुद्धेरात्मा महान् परः ।। १० ।।

महतः परमव्यक्तमव्यक्तात् पुरुषः परः ।
पुरुषान्न परं किञ्चित् सा काष्ठा सा परा गतिः ।। ११ ।।

indiriyebhyaḥ parā hy arthā arthebhyaś ca paraṁ manaḥ ।
manasas tu parā buddhir buddher ātmā mahān paraḥ ।। 10 ।।

mahataḥ param avyaktam avyaktāt puruṣaḥ paraḥ ।
puruṣān na paraṁ kiñcit sā kāṣṭhā sā parā gatiḥ ।। 11 ।।

Beyond senses are their objects,
Beyond sense-objects is mind,
Beyond mind is intellect,
Beyond intellect is the great self. (10)

Beyond the great is the unmanifest,
Beyond the unmanifest is *puruṣa*
Beyond *puruṣa,* none there is.
That is the destination; that is the final refuge. (11)

Leaving aside the chariot analogy, the goal attained is described here in Sāṁkhyan terminology. Sāṁkhya, though one of the six systems of Indian philosophy, due to its preciseness in thinking, had much influenced the other systems, especially Vedānta. Not admitting the *prakṛti-puruṣa* (Nature and Spirit) dualism of Sāṁkhya, Vedānta adapted to its methodology the Sāṁkhyan categorization of the constituent elements of universal and (particular) systems, as early as the time of the Upaniṣads as is evident in the present passages.

What distinguishes the Sāṁkhya system is its admitting two basic realities: *prakṛti* and *puruṣa* (Nature and Spirit). Also called *pradhāna* (the primary source of emanations) and *avyakta* (the unindividuated or the unmanifest), *prakṛti* is the original germ out of which everything evolves. It is beginningless, indestructible, indivisible and limbless. Its existence is to be inferred from its effects. *Puruṣa* (Person or Spirit), on the other hand, is the unevolving witnessing consciousness in each evolved being; there are thus as many *puruṣa*s as there are beings. One not existing without the other, the unitedness of the two, *prakṛti* and *puruṣa*, is also beginningless and endless, an interdependence often compared to that of a lame man travelling on the shoulders of a blind man.

The entire phenomenal world, physical as well as mental, is evolved out of *prakṛti* incited by the three *guṇa*s (*sattva, rajas, tamas*) inherent in itself. Such evolved categories (*tattva*s) are twenty-four in number, and they constitute the world, with *puruṣa* as the twenty-fifth.

Not subscribing to the Sāṁkhyan dualism, Vedānta adopted the *prakṛti* concept, to explain *māyā* the vital force behind the emanation of the world. *Puruṣa* without Sāṁkhyan multiplicity, was equated with the Vedāntic *Brahman*. This way of revaluing the Sāṁkhyan methodology to suit Vedāntic Self-enquiry has been resorted to in the *Bhagavad Gītā* also. The *Gītā,* for example, says,

> The senses, they say, are subtle;
> more subtle than the senses is mind;
> yet finer than mind is intellect;
> that which is beyond even intellect is He. (III.42)

Without detailing the twenty-four categories of the Sāṁkhya system, the present verses simply follow the outline of evolution in its reverse order and show how *Brahman*, the destination of the life-expedition, is beyond all these and equivalent to *puruṣa*.

Though the grades of superiority follows the Sāṁkhyan concept of evolution, the nature of superiority is decided by its nearness to the final goal of Vedānta, and not by nearness to the unevolved state as the Sāṁkhyans conceive it. The *puruṣa*, the interiormost witnessing consciousness, is nothing other than the Self, the essential Substance of our own being.

> एष सर्वेषु भूतेषु गुढोऽऽत्मा न प्रकाशते ।
> दृश्यते त्वग्र्यया बुद्ध्या सूक्ष्मया सूक्ष्मदर्शिभिः ।। १२ ।।
>
> *eṣa sarveṣu bhūteṣu guḍho"tmā na prakāśate* ।
> *dṛśyate tvagryayā buddhyā sūkṣmayā*
> *sūkṣmadarśibhiḥ* ।। 12 ।।
>
> This Self, hidden in all that has come into being, shines not forth. Yet It is perceived by seers of subtlities in their penetrating, subtle, intuitive thinking.

To compare the search for Reality to a charioting expedition may give the impression that the goal is situated somewhere far away to be reached by a long journey. The Self is really not situated at a particular place or point; it is the Substance of the seeker's own being and the Substance of everything. Not having any apparent form, and hence invisible, all apparent forms, tangible or intangible, are assumed for the moment by the non-apparent Self-substance. Imperceptible as it is to the mind and senses, It may be felt to be hiding itself away from the seeker. The seeker, his senses, his mind, his enquiry, are all but mere flickering sparks emanating from that invisible fire. So too is everything. One has only to realize oneself as that Reality, even as an ornament realizes itself as gold; it does not have to go elsewhere to see what is gold, it has only to know itself. Such a self-oriented search for Reality needs an inversion of all the outwardly oriented searching faculties.

> यच्छेद् वाङ् मनसी प्राज्ञ-
> स्तद् यच्छेज्ज्ञान आत्मनि ।
> ज्ञानमात्मनि महति नियच्छेत्
> तद् यच्छेच्छान्त आत्मनि ।। १३ ।।

yacched vāṅ manasī prājñas
tad yacched jñāna ātmani ।
jñānam ātmani mahati niyacchet
tad yacchet śānta ātmani ॥ 13 ॥

A wise one should merge speech in mind, and the latter in the awareness-Self. The awareness should be merged in the Great Self and the Great Self in the Tranquil Self.

The interiorized path of enquiry having been marked out in the last verse, how the enquiry is to be directed along this path is made clear in the present one. Equating each stage of merging with *ātman* (the Self) indicates that nothing is outside the Self. Beginning with speech, the verbal expression of all visual experiences, and ending with the Tranquil Self, beyond speech, the entire range of man's mental faculties is nothing but his Self, himself, self-manifested. This merger of one stage in the next, could be compared to that of one concentric circle in another wider one, all finally merging in the one infinite circle.

उत्तिष्ठत जाग्रत
प्राप्य वरान् निबोधत ।
क्षुरस्य धारा निशिता दुरत्यया
दुर्गं पथस्तत् कवयो वदन्ति ॥ १४ ॥

uittiṣṭhata jāgrata
prāpya varān nibodhata ।
kṣurasya dhārā niśitā duratyayā
durgaṁ pathas tat kavayo vadanti ॥ 14 ॥

Arise Ye! Awake ye! Approaching the best of masters, do get enlightened. Difficult to cross and hard to tread, like a razor's sharpened edge, is that path: so the wise proclaim.

Why is it that the Self, the only Reality, does not get revealed to everyone? Why do we take appearances for real and not enquire into what is behind them, giving rise to all the worries about death? The reason is that we, in the usual course of life, are not fully awake. Why it is so will be clarified at the beginning of the next chapter. What we consider as our wakeful experience is merely a dream. In dream the dream-sight is always taken to be real events; only on waking up from dream do we realize the unrealness of what was seeing till then. So too, that which we treat as real are realized to be mere dream-appearance on waking up from the present dream; till then we go on thinking that all we see are real.

A long dream as it is, we are unlikely to awaken unless stirred awake by someone already awakened. Pleasant as the dream is, we may, even on being called to wake by an awakened one, hesitate to arise, requiring a forceful prod from him. Such an inner urge for rising up wells out at times from oneself, especially on facing certain unresolvable critical situations in life. Though seemingly made to Naciketas, the call here is really meant for us. Naciketas, already entering the mansion of wisdom, needs no further prodding.

Merely becoming aware of the meaninglessness and unrealness of what is perceived does not make one aware of what is real and meaningful, the latter needing the guidance of one who is already enlightened. Such a one has to be approached by the seeker. As Naciketas has already approached Yama himself, this call also is really directed to us. Even a detailed study of scriptures like the present Upaniṣad, along with all the available commentary, would not yield the result intended unless guided by a proper Guru.

More easily said than done; so is it with treading the path of wisdom. A path that demands our all, and where logical reasoning does not work, treading this path is as though walking on a razor's edge. Well-balanced, the feet get cut; on tilting one falls off. Difficult, demanding, and challenging is the path of wisdom, and it must be faced head on, with absolute resoluteness and the help of a proper Guru.

अशब्दमस्पर्शमरूपमव्ययं
तथाऽरसं नित्यमगन्धवच्च यत् ।
अनाद्यनन्तं महतः परं ध्रुवं
निचाय्य तन्मृत्युमुखात् प्रमुच्यते ।। १५ ।।

aśabdam asparśam arūpam avyayaṁ
tathā'rasaṁ nityam agandhavac ca yat ।
anādyanantaṁ mahataḥ paraṁ dhruvaṁ
nicāyya tan mṛtyumukhāt pramucyate ।। 15 ।।

Without sound, without touch, without form, undecaying, without taste, eternal, without smell, without beginning, without end, beyond the Great, stable, (is the Self). Discerning It one is liberated from facing death.

This verse along with the next two, serves as an envoy concluding the chapter which dealt with how the search for the Immortal Self is to be directed, as well as concluding Part I of the upaniṣad. In this chapter we saw how the Substance that assumes the form of oneself is also immortal, and how on realizing it as oneself one becomes immortal, and thus free from death.

The Substance which unfolds itself as the senses as well as their objects, is Itself without senses and therefore it cannot be sensed. The Substance which appears as all the evanescent and unstable forms, It is eternal and stable. The Substance which finds expression as all the measurable entities, is Itself immeasurable — without beginning and end. The Reality that appears as all mortals, Itself is Immortal.

नाचिकेतमुपाख्यानं मृत्युप्रोक्तं सनातनम् ।
उक्त्वा श्रुत्वा च मेधावी ब्रह्मलोके महीयते ।। १६ ।।

nāciketam upākhyānaṁ mr̥tyuproktaṁ sanātanam ।
uktvā śrutvā ca medhāvī brahmaloke mahīyate ।। 16 ।।

This narrative of Naciketas, Death's immemorial teaching — telling it and hearing it, an intelligent one becomes glorified in the *Brahman*-world.

Knowledge of the state after death was what Naciketas desired to learn about. Yama's answer leads him to birthless and deathless Reality, instead of to knowledge of the hereafter. This secret teaching is kept alive even now handed down from generation to generation, an enlightended person teaching an earnest seeker.

As death is an unavoidable part of life, its secrets are always novel wisdom, each seeker acquiring it afresh. This search, unlike in modern science, can never be begun from the point reached by someone else. The secret of death reveals the secret of birth, as it does the secret of life.

It is the enlightenment that one Immortal Reality alone exists; the emergence and merging of phenomenal appearances continually occur in it. Intelligent seekers, instead of identifying themselves with evanescent appearances such as the body, soul and so on, view themselves as not apart from the one Immortal Reality, thus knowing themselves immortal in the *Brahman*-world. The glory of *Brahman* then becomes theirs too, and it is for this reason a *jñānin* (wise one) is always honoured.

य इमं परम गुह्यं
श्रावयेत् ब्रह्मसंसदि ।
प्रयतः श्राद्धकाले वा
तदानन्त्याय कल्पते
तदानन्त्याय कल्पत इति ।। १७ ।।

ya imaṁ paramaṁ guhyaṁ
srāvayet brahma-saṁsadi ।
prayataḥ śrāddha-kāle vā
tad ānantyāya kalpate
tad ānantyāya kalpata iti ।। 17 ।।

Devoutly made heard in an assembly of *Brahman*-seekers or at the ceremony for the dead, this supreme secret makes for everlastingness, makes for everlastingness.

The wise ones, living in the world of *Brahman* as they are, are called brāhmaṇas; as well as *Brahman*-seekers. To such brāhmaṇas, birth and death are unreal, but to the ignorant both are real. They perform propitiatory ritual to honour and appease the departed. However, both the wise and the ignorant, are equally overjoyed when the secret of death is heard — the wise feel joy as their wisdom is confirmed; the joy of the seekers is in knowing the Truth; and the ignorant feel the joy of awakening to a new urge for awareness. To the one who utters these words, it would be the joy of sharing his secret wisdom with his fellow beings, who in essence are not different from himself, the Self. The benefit of imparting this wisdom is thus boundless.

Part II

Chapter I

प्रथमा वल्ली

THE highway leading to Self-knowledge having got cleared in the second section, and the mode of traversing it having been described in the third section of the last chapter, the present section shows how the attainment of the goal is accomplished. It is in intuitive awareness where all dualities get merged in unitiveness — one experiencing the final self-contentment of having attained what was yearned for. This is the *yoga-buddhi* of ancient Indians, and the dialectics of the West.

पराञ्चि खानि व्यतृणत् स्वयम्भू-
स्तस्मात् पराङ् पश्यति नान्तरात्मन् ।
कश्चिद्धीरः प्रत्यगात्मानमैक्ष-
दावृत्तचक्षुरमृतत्वमिच्छन् ।। १ ।।

parāñci khāni vyatr̥ṇat svayambhūḥ
tasmāt parāṅ paśyati nāntarātman ।
kaścid dhīraḥ pratyagātmānam aikṣat
āvr̥ttacakṣur amr̥tatvam icchan ।। 1 ।।

The self-existent (Creator) cut the senses open outward-looking; one, therefore, looks outward, not within himself. Certain wise ones, nevertheless, seeking immortality with eyes interiorized, have seen the indwelling Self.

Life being dear to everyone, no one wishes to die, unless psychological maladjustments induce one to suicide. Death is the most uncertain event in life, while being also the most definite; all of us try to avert it. Man contemplates the crossing over of death. Is it possible, and if so, how?

All beings, by nature, are endowed with the instinctive disposition to avert death, the instinct for self-preservation. Man alone is provided with the thinking habit, in addition to instinct, to achieve this end. One who makes use of this special gift properly, stands by it and imparts its benefits to others is called *dhīra*, which is what the word means etymologically, though it is usually used in referring to a firm and steady person. Most men, though having this natural gift, still live oblivious of it — thus forgoing the benefit of it — guided merely by animal instincts.

Everything apparent is mortal, and every apparent form is conceived as caused by some other apparent form. The cause from where this causal chain originated is a causeless cause, an unoriginated cause, called *svayambhū*, meaning, the self-created, the self-existent, equivalent to the theological concept of God the Creator, the philosophical concept of 'the Absolute', and the scientific concept of 'nature'. To say, therefore, that the Creator created something, indicates that it is so by nature, and there is no other reason adducible. In the context of Indian Mythology, *svayambhū* is an epithet of Brahmā the Creator, where Viṣṇu is the Sustainer and Śiva the Destroyer.

An enigmatic being that he is, man is endowed with two mutually exclusive possibilities in his being. All opening outward and incapable of perceiving themselves, his senses see only objects external. The *ṛṣi* views it as a sort of punishment inflicted on man by the Creator Himself for no apparent reason. However the same Creator has bestowed him with the power of discrimination, the capability to decide for himself the purpose of his living and also the means of accomplishing this purpose, all depending on properly using his nature-given gift of knowledge. Those who are aware of this gift in themselves, transcending the limitations caused by the senses being externally oriented and making use of the very senses, perceive what is Real in themselves. Perceiving the Real, one realizes that the destruction of the body, what we call death, is merely a transformation of the Real from one mode of existence to another — a natural process — and that the Real in oneself does not die at all. As the Real is immortal, when one realizes, 'I am that Real', one experiences oneself as immortal. This Real is the *ātman*/*Brahman* portrayed before as the meaning content of *AUṀ*. Unaware of the immortality of oneself, and guided by the animal needs of begetting, growing, eating and sheltering, the ignorant one takes the perishing of the body as the perishing of oneself, and is worried about the hereafter, as will be explicitly stated in the next verse; whilst an intelligent one, making use of the God-given gift of knowledge, experiences oneness with God, the state known as *sāyujya*.

Everything sense-perceived is external and transient. Capable only of sensing the visible forms and other qualities of objects, the senses do not help us perceive the Reality that appears as all perceived objects as well as all perceiving senses. Eye perceives external forms; it does not see itself. Ear hears external sounds; it does not hear itself. So too with the other senses, because all the senses by nature are turned outward. Tempted by the pleasure offered by external objects, the senses often become a hindrance to the turning of one's attention to the underlying Reality. Once turned inwards and the Reality perceived, the senses, their functions, the pleasures and pains they offer, all are seen as different ways in which Reality finds self-expression. The senses that were a hindrance to Self-knowledge before, become helpful in being able to see for himself how the endless possibilities latent in the Self get unfolded in their own forms.

To turn one's eyes inward does not mean either mechanically turning them inwards, or putting a stop to the natural functions of the senses. One's interest is what matters. Interested in sense-pleasures, one would be tempted to further it; interested in the master-interest of life, attaining immortality, one would withdraw himself naturally from the allurement of sense-pleasures. Interiorization of the eyes, the withdrawal from sense pleasures, thus always has to be accompanied and complemented by the yearning for immortality, one supporting and invigorating the other.

पराचः कामाननुयन्ति बाला-
स्ते मृत्योर्यन्ति विततस्य पाशम् ।
अथ धीरा अमृतत्वं विदित्वा
ध्रुवमध्रुवेष्विह न प्रार्थयन्ते ।। २ ।।

parācaḥ kāmān anuyanti bālāḥ
te mṛtyor yanti vitatasya pāśam ।
atha dhīra amṛtatvaṁ viditvā
dhruvam adhruveṣv iha na prārthayante ॥ 2 ॥

The childish, going after external pleasures, walk into the widespread snare of death. The wise, however, discerning immortality, seek not the stable among the unstable here.

As the habit of becoming enamoured of colourful objects, is a part of children's life, those who persue sense-pleasures are described as children (*bālāḥ*) in Sanskrit, and the word has become almost a synonym for the ignorant. Interested in one thing for a moment, leaving it to go after another the next, is common to both children and the ignorant. Carried away by momentary pleasures, both are oblivious of the immortal Reality which they are, Happiness (*ānanda*) itself in essence.

Desirable objects are countless in number and variety, and those who pursue them come to a point where they cannot chase after pleasures any further, though desire still persists. Instead of the further prospect of enjoying life what one sees then is impending death. Ignorant of the immortal Reality one is, one doubts: will I cease to exist on the event of death, or will I be reborn to enjoy or suffer the fruits of my actions? Unable to find a convincing answer, one feels caught in an inescapable trap, unless and until the immortal Self-Reality in oneself is realized. Realizing the Self, one finds the trap vanished and oneself free and immortal. What we call birth and death are part of the phenomenal becoming, ceaselessly taking place in the one Immortal Self. Those who are desirous of immortality, therefore, would never search for it among mortal appearances, but would try to find the way to go beyond them.

Not knowing one's own immortality and taking oneself as mortal is thus equal to killing oneself, and therefore the ignorant are sometimes called self-killers (*ātma-hantā*) as in the *Īśa Upanisad* (Verse 3) ; here they are merely treated as children.

येन रूपं रसं गन्धं शब्दान् स्पर्शांश्च मैथुनान् ।
एतेनैव विजानाति किमत्र परिशिष्यते ।
एतद् वै तत् ॥ ३ ॥

yena rūpaṁ rasaṁ gandhaṁ śabdān sparśāṁś ca maithunān ।
etenaiva vijānāti kim atra pariśiṣyate ।
etad vai tat ॥ 3 ॥

This apart, because of which alone form, taste, smell, sound, touch, sexual union, all are perceived, what else is here? This verily is That.

If not to be found among perishing objects, where is the Imperishable, then to be found? The answer is given here:

We perceive objects; we enjoy them; we think of their origin; we even conceive ideas of their origin — all as varying functions of one ivariable Consciousness. This Consciousness (*cit*), along with *sat* (Existence) and *ānanda* (Value-experience) is not merely a specifying quality of the Self; these three as one is the essential content of the Self, the Immortal Reality. As *sat* It exists; as *cit* It is conscious of Itself and of everything that emanates from It (nothing in this world exists other than what emanates from the one Reality); as *ānada* It creates and feels all pleasures and pains. As *sat-cit*, It exists and is aware of the infinite potential latent in Itself, and in its insurmountable urge to actualize it, It unfolds itself assuming the form of all objects and subjects, all perceptual experiences, and the pleasures and pains that go with them. It perceives (*vijānāti*) all these as happening within Itself. Nothing else exists anywhere, any way, any time, other than as some form or other of the one and only Self-Reality. It, in fact, perceives nothing 'other'; it always perceives Itself. Though it happens every moment in our life, this truth remains hidden from us due to our childishness. The Reality within oneself, the Reality that has assumed the form of oneself, the Immortal Reality one is ever in search of — knowing It one feels, 'What else does remain to be known!' Even a simple sense-perception, once the Reality underlying it is perceived, could be instrumental in leading us to real Self-perception, the perception of oneself as the immortal Self.

The word *tat* (That) of the last line of the verse stands for *Brahman* as the final goal of all enquiry, as against the world indicated by the word 'here' (*atra*) of the line before. It is this 'That' which was previously cited in Verse I.ii.15 as a *brahmacārin*'s goal, as the secret taught in all the Vedas, and the Reality talked about by all who lead austere life — the mystical meaning of *AUṀ*, what Naciketas saw within the mansion!

स्वप्नान्तं जागरितान्तं चोभौ येनानुपश्यति ।
महान्तं विभुमात्मानं मत्वा धीरो न शोचति ।। ४ ।।

svapnāntaṁ jāgaritāntaṁ cobhau yenānupaśyati ।
mahāntaṁ vibhum ātmānaṁ matvā dhīro na
śocati ।। 4 ।।

By whom the two — the bounds of sleep and the bounds of wakefulness — are perceived together, he knows that *Ātman* the Great. Such a wise one grieves not.

Elucidating the vision of the last verse, the present one portrays the Self as the Consciousness that witnesses all the altering states of consciousness. It is the *Māṇḍūkya Upaniṣad* that compartmentalizes the states of consciousness into four: *jāgarita* (waking state), *svapna* (dreaming state), *suṣupti* (deep sleep), the *truīya* (the fourth, the mystical experience of non-duality). Compartmentalized thus for the sake of making it easier to study though, the altering states of consciousness are not easy to compartmentalize. No one knows when one slips from one state to another. It would also be difficult to classify such states as day-dreaming, as dream or wakeful experience. As the state of total wakefulness is not known to anyone, no one has ever experienced it, and none can say what it is like. An element of sleepiness always is present in what we consider wakeful experience. Only the degree of sleepiness or wakefulness varies. In what we call the waking state, we at times feel fully alert and at other times drowsy. So too with deep sleep; nothing is known of that state. Having no defining characteristic, *suṣupti* (deep sleep) also remains ununderstandable; so no one can claim to have had that experience either. Both complete wakefulness and deep sleep are thus neither fully known nor fully attained by anyone. In our actual living what we do experience is an oscillation of consciousness between these extremes, like the pendulum of a clock, never touching either extreme, *jāgarita* or *svapna*. (The word *svapna*, though usually translated as dream, originally means sleep.) The altering states of consciousness is portrayed here by just mentioning the two extremes, with no reference to any of the states in between. This particular way was preferred by Narayana Guru also, in all his speculations on the subject.

The one Consciousness that assumes the form of and oscillates between the two extreme states of wakefulness (*jāgaritāntam*) and deep sleep (*svapnāntam*) is the Self. It is not merely an animating principle, as is usually conceived; it is the substantial reality, the knowing consciousness and the experience of enjoying, all in one.

Realizing oneself as that Immortal Self, one would not be grieved by the thought of death and the state thereafter.

The Self which is the Reality underlying the enquiring mind, is not accessible to it, and any mind that attempts to grasp It would therefore feel overwhelmed by its mysterious greatness. Which is why, instead of pursuing It, the mind would rather glorify Its greatness: this being the rationale behind the worshipful attitude of man. The epithet 'the Great' (*mahāntam*) implies also that it is the adorable one.

God, in religious sense, is always thought of as the omnipresent (*vibhu*). The Absolute, the Self, the all-pervading Substance, is also omnipresent in the ontological sense.

य इमं मध्वदं वेद आत्मानं जीवमन्तिकात् ।
ईशानं भूतभव्यस्य न ततो विजुगुप्सते ।
एतद् वै तत् ।। ५ ।।

ya imaṁ madhvadaṁ veda ātmānaṁ jīvam
antikāt ।
īśānaṁ bhūta-bhavyasya na tato vijugupsate ।
etad vai tat ।। 5 ।।

One who knows close at hand the honey-eater, the individuated being, as the Self, the lord of the past and the future, he would not desire to protect himself from It. This verily is That.

Here we are being led towards a new aspect of the Self, on the basis of yet another etymological derivation of the word *ātman*: its individuated aspect as enjoyer of everything. One derivation of the word having been explained under Verse I.ii.20, the present sense is derived from the root *ad* (to eat, to enjoy), giving a sense more psychological in significance while the former was ontological. Happiness, compared here with honey (*madhu*), is the impelling force behind all human endeavour. It need not always be a pleasant experience, pain also is life-nourishing. To feel the lack of something is painful, and this pain and the desire to alleviate it induces one to make efforts. The expectation of actualizing more enduring values is what makes life worth living. All that makes our existence and endeavours meaningful could well be likened to honey. The *Bṛhadāraṇyaka Upaniṣad*, using the honey analogy, teaches how such honey-like values could be strung in a graded fashion culminating in the honey-eating of Self-Happiness.

At the earth-earthy level, earth is honey for all beings and all beings honey for the earth, one necessary for making the existence of the other meaningful and even possible. The universal reality of earth assumes the form of body in each being. The one luminous (*tejomaya*) and immortal (*amṛtamaya*) principle (*puruṣa*) that makes each honey for the other, is the Self, is *Brahman*, is the Immortal, is everything here. The honey and the honey-eater thus transcended, one attains the status of the non-dual Self. The *BṛhadāraṇyakaUpaniṣad* thus begins to reveal the non-dual Reality with the earth and human body for its dual aspects of existence, the former universal and the latter individual. It thus goes on to show how the same could be attained at other gradually ascending, subtler levels of existence — water, fire, air, the sun, the directions, the moon, lightning, thunder, space,righteousness, truth, man and finally the Self — each of which is considered honey for all living beings and all living beings honey for it.

Gold-substance, individuated, assumes the form of various ornaments. Similarly individuated Self-Substance assumes the form of living beings, each called a *jīva*. *Jīva*, commonly understood as esquivalent to 'soul', strictly speaking is any individual being that survives through breathing, as its etymological derivation indicates: (*jīva-prāṇa-dhāraṇe*). The Immortal honey-eater, the Self, is the Substance that gets manifested as all individual beings, including the seeker. The seeker can therefore only realize the Self as his own being, the *jīva*. The entity nearest to any being is none other than its own substance, thus the Self is the reality nearest (*antikāt*) to everyone.

Without beginning and end, the individuating process goes on in the Immortal Self-Substance, every individuated form giving place to one or more new ones, all together creating the impression of the existence of the world. This unceasing flow of events is divided by the human mind into past and the future, with that point in time called the present between the two. In our actual experience, on the other hand, only the present exists; it continues endlessly; the past being merely the present memory of the events gone, and the future our present hopes and expectations of events yet to come. This flow of events, indivisible as the past, present and future, consisting of emanation of new individual forms, called birth, and the disappearance of old forms, called death, like the appearance and disappearance of waves in an ocean, has an order of its own, though inconceivable to the human mind. What is conceivable, though, is that it is effected by the consciousness (*cit*) aspect of the Self. The Self, understood in this way as the controller of the world, is called *Īśvara* or *Īśa*, equivalent to the theological concept of God.

By instinct we abhor death and try to save ourselves from it at whatever cost. Nevertheless, one who is aware of the Self-Substance in oneself and of Its immortality, treats the so-called death merely as the merger of a wave in the Immortal ocean of the Self. The original word *na vijugupsate* can be construed as either 'does not desire to protect' or 'does not detest'. Socrates puts the same thoughts in a poetical way: Since the real philosopher is already dead he sees what is called death only as the last phase of the realization of Truth. This is what Naciketas visualized within the mansion!

यः पूर्वं तपसो जातमद्भ्यः पूर्वमजायत ।
गुहां प्रविश्य तिष्ठन्तं यो भूतेभिर्व्यपश्यत ।
एतद् वै तत् ।। ६ ।।

yaḥ pūrvaṁ tapaso jātaṁ adbhyaḥ pūrvam ajāyata ।
guhāṁ praviśya tiṣṭhantaṁ yo bhutebhir vyapaśyata ।
etad vai tat ।। 6 ।।

> That which in the beginning brought forth the world from Itself through *tapas*, was existing even before the emergence of waters; It abides entering the secret abode; It beheld itself through the beings emerged — This verily is That.

To ask, 'What is it?', 'Who made it?', 'How was it made?', 'Why was it made?' is natural with man on seeing something new. In Vedānta the 'What', 'Who', 'How', and 'Why' of the ever new phenomenon of life are all answered in terms of the Self. The self-existing Substance, *ātman*, *sat*, as *cit* or Consciousness, thought: 'Let me be born as many', and was induced to do so in the hope of actualizing its own *ānanda* (Happiness) content through self-expression. This Upaniṣadic concept of Creation, analogous to birds' hatching from eggs, is a self-heating process called *tapas*, meaning heat, as is elaborated in Chapter I of the *Aitareya Upaniṣad*. Water was considered as the phenomenon that emerged first, probably symbolizing the water-like nature of all genetic matter. This Creation story, told for the satisfaction those who think in terms of a temporal origin of the world, is meant to be understood rather symbolically. However, it is a known fact that making of something new requires a lot of brooding on the part of the maker, and some form of heating of the raw material is also part of the process of giving a new shape to something; both these are *tapas*. The self-existing Self, too, brooding over the world to be created of Itself, underwent a self-heating process in order to transform Itself as the world. The Reality we are in search of is that Substance which underwent this self-unfolding *tapas*. The Self is the Reality that existed even before the emergence of the first phenomenon of water, if at all a gradual evolution of the world is taken for granted.

Man, an end-result of this self-heating of the Self, in order to realize what he really is, needs to undergo the same *tapas*, the well-known self-disciplined austere way of living of seekers. The *tapas* undergone by the seeker, is thus the regression of the *tapas* undergone by the primeval Substance, the Self, to create him.

How the Self is felt to be hiding unknown, somewhere, has already been discussed under Verse I.ii.20.

Concluding the Creation story, the *Aitareya Upaniṣad* says, the Self looked at everything thus created, but could only see Itself in everything (I. i. 13). The Self was seeing Itself in and through all beings; so too, one who knows the Self sees himself in and through all beings. He sees himself in everything, and everything in himself, as the *Īśa Upaniṣad* puts it. The Self we are in search of is nothing but the one substance in ourselves and in everything; it appears as oneself and as everything; and thus the Reality is realized as oneself and as everything. That is the Reality Naciketas saw within the mansion!

या प्राणेन संभवत्यदितिर्देवतामयी ।
गुहां प्रविश्य तिष्ठन्तीं या भूतेभिर्व्यजायत ।
एतद् वै तत् ।। ७ ।।

yā prāṇena sambhavaty aditir devatāmayī ।
guhāṁ pravisya tiṣṭhantīṁ yā bhūtebhir vyajāyāta ।
etad vai tat ।। 7 ।।

Aditi, the one who emerges from *prāṇa,* and of the essence of divinity, who abides entering the secret abode, who was born along with beings — this verily is That.

All that arises from the one Self-Substance, all together represented by Aditi in this verse, is seen here as not different from the Self in essence, even as an ornament is not different from gold in essence, the effect having no existence apart from that of the cause. The causal Substance, in order to emanate all things from it, needs to be a vital one, a breathing, pulsating one, and so it is *prāṇa* in this context, meaning that which breathes, pulsates and lives. Aditi, representing all that emerges, means 'the inexhaustible and boundless', signifying the boundlessness of phenomenal becoming. The word also means earth, the grossest of the entities that emerge. Aditi thus signifies all aspects of manifestation, from the causal vitality to the grossest appearance of matter. Mythologically, Aditi is the mother of all heavenly beings, gods or *devas*. *Devas*, as beings are effulgence in essence, and stand for all that arises in consciousness — ideas and mental images, again inexhaustible and boundless. Aditi thus represents everything that arises from one primeval source, physically as well as mentally, both together constituting the world. Aditi and the world together, have no existence apart from the Self, and is the Self.

The origination of everything from one source, is too mysterious to be comprehensible, and therefore Aditi as a representation of this cause is worshipped rather than comprehended. Aditi thus gained the status of a deity worthy of worship (*devatā*) or rather the status of the representative of all deities. The word *devatā*, also means that which is effulgence in essence. The mysterious conscious function behind every phenomenal becoming is a *devatā*, a worshippable deity. Aditi, representing all *devatā*s, thus becomes *devatāmayī* (the essence or sum total of all worshippable entities). The mysteriousness of the origin of everything makes us feel that Aditi too hides in a secret abode as does the Self, the *prāṇa*.

The birth of Aditi means the birth of everything; the birth of Aditi is thus along with the birth of all beings, one meaningless without the other, both but different facets of the one and only birth.

The Self, in its emergence as comprehensible to us, though in an incomprehensible manner — assuming the form of Aditi and the world — is the Reality we are in search of. That is the Reality Naciketas visualizes within the mansion!

अरण्योर्निहितो जातवेदा गर्भ इव सुभृतो गर्भिणीभिः ।
दिवे दिव ईड्यो जागृवद्भिर्हविष्मद्भिर्मनुष्येभिरग्निः ।
एतद् वै तत् ॥ ८ ॥

araṇyor nihito jātavedā garbha iva subhṛto
garbhiṇībhiḥ ।
dive diva īḍyo jāgṛvadbhir haviṣmadbhir
manuṣyebhir agniḥ ।
etad vai tat ॥ 8 ॥

The Fire, hiding in the pair of fire-sticks, like an embryo well-cared-for by a pregnant woman, is to be adored with oblations day after day by the heedful, and is to be preserved by them. This verily is That.

According to the Vedic custom, the two fire-sticks called *araṇi,* cut from the same three, are to be rubbed together to kindle the sacrifical fire.

It is a must that strict ritualists keep this fire alive at home day in and day out. So too the fire of Self-knowledge is to be kept alive by the seeker of wisdom as well as by the enlightened. What is accomplished here is a revaluation and sublimation of the ritualistic concept of maintaining the sacrifical fire, to fit in with the wisdom context of Vedānta.

Fire is the one that carries oblations to gods, in return for favours; the fire of wisdom is the means of attaining the final goal — liberation. Fire, hiding in the fire-sticks, when kindled, can consume even the very fire-sticks; the fire of wisdom consumes its own source, the individual being with all physical and mental faculties, which when rubbed together give rise to enlightenment. Subject and object, emerging from the one Self-Reality, when rubbed together, causes enlightenment, which consumes subjects, objects, as well as the entire world.

The original word *jātavedas* for fire, means the one who knows everything born. The Self, the Substance of everything born, also knows everything born. A ritualist cares for maintaining the sacrificial fire, like pregnant woman does for the pregnancy she carries within, which makes her existence joyful, her life purposeful. So too is the care of a seeker for the wisdom he is in search of; so too is the care of a *jñānin* for the wisdom he has acquired; both consider wisdom the one thing that makes life purposeful and joyful.

Though alternately emerging and dying out, the fire principle never ceases to exist; so too is the fire of the Self. A pregnant woman sees that which makes her life meaningful, within herself; the seeker seeks what he does within himself. The meaning content he sees within is the meaning content in everything without. Unable to comprehend it, he feels, it is a mystery, and thus feels like worshipping it. Once comprehended, everything loses its wonder. So much so good that the Self remains ever ununderstandable. Such is the Self within, that we are in search of. Such is the Reality Naciketas sees within the mansion!

यतश्चोदेति सूर्योऽस्तं यत्र च गच्छति ।
तं देवाः सर्वेऽर्पितास्तदु नात्येति कश्चन ।
एतद् वै तत् ।। ९ ।।

yataś codeti suryo'staṁ yatra ca gacchati ।
taṁ devāḥ sarve'rpitās tad u nātyeti kaścana ।
etad vai tat ।। 9 ।।

> Whence the Sun rises, and where it goes to rest — on It are all gods founded; and no one goes beyond It. This verily is That.

The Sun, the most effulgent entity visible in this world, must have had, atleast for the sake of argument, an original source, a source that emanates effulgence and re-absorbs it. That original source is none other than the Self.

The most immense energy source for the entire living world where alone death occurs, is the Sun. Man, one among innumerable kinds of living beings, worries about death and the state after. Man, and all living beings, even the Sun that invigorates everything, have their original source in the Self, the birthless and deathless Reality, absolute effulgence in essence. It is this one Reality that unfolds itself as the world with a structural coherence of its own in which life goes on without beginning and end in and through the cyclic process of birth, life and death of individual beings. Aware of this source and seeing It in oneself, one would not be worried about either death or the state after death, because one knows that the Self alone exists always.

The worlds of gods (*deva*s) and of manes (*pitṛ*s) are sometimes thought of as the hereafter. If at all those worlds and their inhabitants do exist, they must also have originated from the same source, the Self, as did this world; and must also be of the same Self-Substance as this world is, and not different from That. The here and the hereafter, man and gods, all have emanated from, and are pervaded by the one causal Reality, the Self. The Awareness of being one with That makes the question of the hereafter vanish. One Reality alone exists both here and in the hereafter, and is beyond the duality of the here and the hereafter, as is more explicitly stated in the next verse. Nothing exists beyond That; nothing is to be sought for beyond That; no one goes beyond That, as no one goes beyond oneself. This Self, oneself and the all-pervading Self, is the Reality we are in search of.

It is this Reality Naciketas saw within the mansion!

यदेवेह तदमुत्र यदमुत्र तदन्विह ।
मृत्योः स मृत्युमाप्नोति य इह नानेव पश्यति ।। १० ।।

yadeveha tad amutra yad amutra tad anviha ।
mṛtyoḥ sa mṛtyum āpnoti ya iha nāneva
paśyati ॥ 10 ॥

Whatever is here, that is hereafter; what is hereafter, that again is here. Who perceives as though the two are different, he goes from death to death.

Based on what was stated in the last verse, this one differentiates the perceptions of the ignorant and the wise. He who sees one Self-Reality alone in all the worlds, is the wise one; for him the problem of leaving one and reaching another does not arise at all. The ignorant, not perceiving the all-pervading Self, sees the many worlds as real, and treat death as the event of leaving this world. Leaving one world means reaching another, to be born there or somewhere else. To be reborn means to die again. This cyclic process called *saṁsāra* is considered real by the ignorant. They feel they undergo this process, for the nature of the world as well as the nature of life is as one perceives it. The ignorant perceive it wrongly and think birth and death are real, and so they experience them as real as well, as will be made more explicit in the next verse. Whether one is in *saṁsāra* or simply remains unborn and unceasing depends, thus, on how one perceives oneself and the world of which one is an integral part.

मनसैवेदमाप्तवयं नेह नानास्ति किञ्चन ।
मृत्योः स मृत्युं गच्छति य इह नानेव पश्यति ।। ११ ।।

manasaivedam āptavayaṁ neha nānāsti kiñcana ।
mrtyoḥ sa mṛtyuṁ gacchati ya iha nāneva
paśyati ॥ 11 ॥

By intuititive mind indeed one perceives
That many do not exist at all;
One who perceives many as existing,
He goes from death to death.

It is our mind, our thinking, our understanding, that shapes our life. Wrong perception by a deluded mind, makes illusory appearance seem real. Right perception by an undeluded mind, makes the Real appear as real.

The Self, Consciousness (*cit*) in essence, manifests as everything apparent, and thus all appearances are *cit* in essence. Mind, one of such functional facets of *cit*, perceives other such functional facets as objects, and they appear in accordance with the colouring of the mind and its likes and dislikes, not as they really are. A jaundiced eye seeing the world as yellowish does not mean that the world really is yellow. Thinking of the world as matter in essence, one sees only a material world; thinking of the world as the Self in essence, one sees only the Self appearing as the world. The world perceived depends on the perceiving mind.

The apparent many do not cease to appear even on intuitively perceiving the one Reality. Those who see the many apparent manifestations in the one Reality, and the one Reality manifesting as many, are the real seers, the true philosophers.

अङ्गुष्ठमात्रः पुरुषो मध्य आत्मनि तिष्ठति ।
ईशानो भूतभव्यस्य न ततो विजुगुप्सते ।
एतद् वै तत् ॥ १२ ॥

aṅguṣṭha-mātraḥ puruṣo madhya ātmani tiṣṭhati ।
īśāno bhūta-bhavyasya na tato vijugupsate ।
etad vai tat ॥ 12 ॥

Puruṣa, the size of a thumb, resides as the core of one's own being. The Lord of the past and the future, Him one would not desire to save oneself from.

The four verses of the rest of this chapter, bringing in the Vedic concept of *puruṣa*, are aids to meditative perception of the Self-Reality rather than a description of the perception as such. The word *purusa*, used in the sense of 'person', literally means 'dweller of the city' (*pure śayati iti*). Every individual organism is like a city, and has *puruṣa*, Consciousness, conscious of itself as 'I', for its core. The city of the entire cosmos has for its *puruṣa*, the core Consciousness known as God (*Īśa*), meaning the indwelling controller. The non-dual *puruṣa* is the one Consciousness that functions in an individual organism as the I-sense and in the cosmos as *Īśa*.

It is not as if the *puruṣa* is seated at a particular central point either of the body or of the cosmic system. Such a point conceivable is the knowing consciousness itself. *Puruṣa*'s centrality is as this consciousness. Conceiving the Self as spatially located would be in violation of Its all-pervasiveness. Yet meditating It as a non-flickering flame of the size of a thumb is considered by some as helpful for seekers — at times to be meditated as the focal point (*hr̥t*) of one's own being, at other times as situated between the eyebrows, or even as located ten inches from the tip of one's nose. Such differences indicate the seeker's preference for a particular way of meditating. It in no way affects the Self-Reality attained.

All that has been in the past are now dead; all that will be in the future is yet to be born; all that is present is already born, but yet to die. This incessant process of birth, life and death does not take place in a chaotic way. Forming a cosmos (meaning an ordered system), it has a structural integrity of its own, though felt at times as being very unpleasant and incovenient to human sentiments and values. Unknown to man, though, it is a system. Every system is systematized by a conscious mind. The universal consciousness that keeps up the living existences of the cosmos is called *Īśa*, the indwelling controller. The past, the future, the present, are part of the systematic emanation of this one *Īśa,* the Self.

Seeing oneself as that *Īśa*, the birthless and deathless *puruṣa*, one is freed from the fear of death which simply is the event of the wave merging back in the ocean of *Īśa*. That *Īśa*, that *puruṣa*, is the Self we are in search of, and is the Reality perceived by Naciketas inside the mansion!

अङ्गुष्ठमात्रः पुरुषो ज्योतिरिवाधूमकः ।
ईशानो भूतभव्यस्य स एवाद्य स उ श्वः ।
एतद् वै तत् ।। १३ ।।

aṅguṣṭha-mātraḥ puruṣo jyotir ivādhūmakaḥ ।
īśāno bhūta-bhavyasya sa evādya sa u śvaḥ ।
etad vai tat ।। 13 ।।

Puruṣa, the size of a thumb, like a smokeless flame, the lord of the past and the future, alone exists today, alone will exist tomorrow. This verily is That.

The person of the size of thumb can be meditated on as a smokeless flame. It does not cease to exist at any point in time. It exists today, will exist tomorrow and for ever.

Smoke, emerging from fire, clouds its own brightness; likewise, ignorance arising from consciousness along with the resultant conditionings, veils its own transparency. Such conditioning factors, ever changing, cause the appearance of various stages in life, six in number: *asti* (existence), *janma* (birth), *vṛddhi* (growth), *pariṇāma* (evolution), *apakṣaya* (degeneration), *vināśa* (dissolution), whilst the Self remains ever changeless.

It is such ever changing appearance, experienced as constant events, that creates time sense. If there are no events, there is no time-consciousness, of which notions of today, tomorrow and so on are all a part. The here and the hereafter, temporally understood, are today and tomorrow. What exists ever is the Self alone, the Reality that Naciketas perceives within the mansion!

यथोदकं दुर्गे वृष्टं पर्वतेषु विधावति ।
एवं धर्मान् पृथक् पश्यंस्तानेवानुविधावति ।। १४ ।।

yathodakaṁ durge vṛṣṭaṁ parvateṣu vidhāvati ।
evam dharmān pṛthak paśyaṁs tān
evānuvidhāvati ।। 14 ।।

Water rained in ravines runs to waste among hills; so too he who sees qualities as existing on their own runs to waste after them.

On perceiving an object, for instance a rose, what we sense directly are its qualities: the colour shape, fragrance, softness and so on in the case of a rose. The rose as such, the qualified, remains unperceived. Every perceptual experience we have of an object is therefore merely a mental construct. Our world experience also is thus a mental construct, what we directly perceive of it are all its qualities, the qualified Reality always remaining unperceived. All perceived qualities are attributes of some substance, always impereptible. The world and its countless qualitiess are attribute of the imperceptible Self-Substance.

The perceptible qualities of a rose do not exist apart from the imperceptible rose; the perceptible world and its qualities, all attributed to the Self, do not exist apart from the Self. The qualities or attributes are called *dharmas* and the qualified, the substance, *dharmin*. Never existing separately, their distinctness is a mere conceptualization and causes all the worries of life, death the severest of them all. Birth and death, not affecting the Substance in any way, appear in the realm of attributes alone; realizing them as having no existence apart from the Substance, and the Substance as birthless and deathless, releases one from all worries of death.

In our day-to-day life our concern is always for the attributes, causing the feeling that life is dissipated and scattered with all its trials and tribulations, as with water rained in a ravine.

Realizing the imperceptible Substance, one attains the unity of the Self, as stated in the next verse.

यथोदकं शुद्धे शुद्धमासिक्तं तादृगेव भवति ।
एवं मुनेर्विजानत आत्मा भवति गौतम ।। १५ ।।

yathodakaṁ śuddhe śuddham āsiktaṁ tādṛg eva bhavati ।
evaṁ muner vijānāta atmā bhavati gautama ।। 15 ।।

As pure water poured forth into pure water becomes the very same, so is the Self, O Gautama, of the silent seer who knows.

A drop of pure water, dropped into pure water, merges with it losing its identity. An individual, a seeker, knowing himself as the Self, becoming as transparent as clear water, is dropped into the clear-water-ocean of the Self, loses his identity; loosing his voice too, he becomes silent, a *muni*, his experience inexpressible!

Perceiving the one Substance intuitively, all attributes, death included, lose their identity. What exists then is the Self alone!

This is the experience Naciketas had inside the mansion!

Chapter II

द्वितीया वल्ली

पुरमेकादशद्वारमजस्यावक्रचेतसः ।
अनुष्ठाय न शोचति विमुक्तश्च विमुच्यते ।
एतद् वै तत् ।। १ ।।

puram ekādaśa-dvāram ajasyāvakra-cetasaḥ ।
anuṣṭhāya na śocati vimuktaś ca vimucyate ।
etad vai tat ।। 1 ।।

The eleven-gated city belongs to One unborn of upright mind — adhering to Him one grieves not; freed of grief, one becomes liberated. This verily is That.

THE last chapter dealt with how the non-dual, Immortal Self is realized transcending all dualities. The present one centres around how the one Immortal Self, the unborn, assumes the multiple appearances. While in the previous chapter thought was of an ascending order, going from the many appearances to the one Reality, here it is the other way around, one becoming many. The distinction between the two, though subtle, is of decisive importance in Vedāntic methodology where seeing one in many and many in one are equally significant. The oft-repeated words *etad vai tat* (This verily is That) appearing in both the chapters, indicate that the two belong together as mutually compensatory and mutually cancellable. Multiplicity of appearance in no way affects the unity of Reality and *vice versa*, even as the multiplicity of ornaments in no way affects the unity of gold. Gold and ornaments are inseparably one; so too the Self and the world are inseparably one. Similar is the duality of mind and matter, body and soul.

Though usually considered a city of nine gates — two eyes, two ears, two nostrils, two excretory orifices, and mouth — here the human body is said to be a city of eleven gates, the navel and *vidṛti* (sagittal siture) added. What counts here is not the exact number of gates, but rather the stress on multiplicity of appearances emanating from one Substance.

Born as everything, the Self is the unborn *sat*. In knowing which appearances are to be born, and how they are to be born, It is *cit* (Consciousness). Its way of giving birth to everything, Its way of programming everything, is upright, not motivated by any particular interest, and it advances uninterrupted. Man thinks and plans, on the other hand, motivated by interests in personal gains and sentiments, and hence his mind mostly becomes perverted.

To make one's own existence conforming to the unfoldment of Self is what one needs to do to make life happy and fearless. The word *anuṣṭhāya* is interpretable in two ways: as 'on meditating' and as 'on making one's own existence in conformity with something'. To make self-existence in conformity with Self-Reality and Its upright unfoldment is the best possible meditation (*anuṣṭhāna*). One who meditates thus sees only the Self in the various functions of one's own gates, in the functions of the world, in the ups and downs of life's progress, and in all emergence and merger of apparent forms. Seeing only the Self in oneself and everywhere, one sees that there is nothing to be worried about, nothing to be feared, nothing to be grieved over. Free from griefs, and one with the Self, he is the liberated one, he is already within the mansion, already part of the mansion.

हंसः शुचिषद् वसुरन्तरिक्षसद्
होता वेदिषदतिथिर्दुरोणसत् ।
नृषद् वरसदृतसद् व्योमसदब्जा गोजा
ऋतजा अद्रिजा ऋतं बृहत् ।। २ ।।

haṁsaḥ śuciṣad vasur antarikṣasad
hotā vediṣad atithir duroṇasat ।
nṛṣad varasad ṛtasad vyomasad abjā gojā
ṛtajā adrijā ṛtaṁ bṛhat ।। 2 ।।

> It appears like a swan in the clear (like the Sun in the sky), the Vasu in the atmosphere, priest at the altar, guest in the house. It dwells in man, in gods, in the world order (*ṛta*), in the sky. It is all that is born of water, born of earth, born of the world-order, born of mountains. It is the True, It is the Great.

This verse, an almost verbatim repetition of a famous Vedic one, declares that, whatever the variety of appearances — here or in the hereafter, the qualified or the qualities, the one or the many, subtle or gross, mind or matter, cause or effect — all emerge of one *ātman*/*Brahman* and all are the same Self in essence.

The word *haṁsa* is construable as swan, the sun or the Supreme Self. *Vasu* could be taken as meaning light-rays, water or that which moves above. So too *atithiḥ duroṇasat* is interpretable as the earthen jar containing the sacrificial *soma* juice or a guest at home. *Rta* is similarly a word of multiple significance: righteousness, truth, the world-order, sacrifice, the results of sacrifice and so on.

ऊर्ध्वं प्राणमुन्नयत्यपानं प्रत्यगस्यति ।
मध्ये वामनमासीनं विश्वे देवा उपासते ।। ३ ।।

ūrdhvaṁ prāṇam unnayatyapānaṁ pratyag asyati
madhye vāmanam āsīnaṁ viśve devā upāsate ।। 3 ।।

> It is the one that leads *prāṇa* upwards.
> It is the one that brings down *apāna*.
> It is the one seated in the middle as worthy of adoration.
> It is the one all the gods (senses) adore.

Cosmic functions having been seen in the previous verse as pervaded and controlled by the Self, this verse claims the same with regard to the functions of individual organisms. Conceiving of the biological vital functions that keep up an organism living, the ancient *ṛṣis* divided them into five: *prāṇa*, *apāna*, *vyāna*, *udāna*, *samāna*. Though *prāna* as a generic term refers to all the five functions together, it denotes out-breath as a specific function, and *apāna* is its opposite, though the details of the functions of each are veriously conceived by various interpreters of different schools. The *Praśna Upaniṣad*, in Chapter III, makes a detailed analysis of these five functions as manifestations of the Self. A study of it followed by intense cogitation could well be recommended here. Such functions, voluntary as well as involuntary, go on uninterrupted till the moment of the last breath. It is the *sat* aspect of the Self that exists and functions as these systems, the *cit* aspect that is aware of the 'how' and 'why' of the functions, and the *ānanda* aspect, making use of them, actualizes contentment. Representative of these five, only the first two are mentioned here as facets of self-expression of the Self-Substance.

The senses, are conceived as *devas* (gods) in many of the Upaniṣads, as all of them are outlets of the brightness of consciousness, and function as they do because of the programming and functioning of the Self, and therefore all of them are rather poetically imagined as paying homage to the Self. Once the Self ceases to function in an organism, the vital functions and the senses all cease to exist. The *Praśna Upaniṣad*, takes this as a major issue for discussion.

The non-dual Self, that expresses itself as the cosmic system and as the individual system, is the meaning content of *AUṀ* mentioned earlier when Yama began his teaching (see Chapter II of Part I). Controller and controlled being undifferentiated, the subject itself being the object of its knowing, the only way to know It is through the intuitive perception, of meditation, where subject and object merge in the being of the Self, and meditation and adoration also become inseparable. That which is perceived in this manner is given the epithet *vāmana*, meaning, worthy of being adored and served, though in ordinary literature it denotes any diminutive being. However, this sense indirectly suggests the minuteness of the Self.

अस्य विस्त्रंसमानस्य शरीरस्थस्य देहिनः ।
देहाद् विमुच्यमानस्य किमत्र परिशिष्यते ।
एतद् वै तत् ।। ४ ।।

asya visraṁsamānasya śarīrasthasya dehinaḥ ।
dehād vimucyamānasya kim atra pariśiṣyate ।
etad vai tat ।। 4 ।।

When the embodied that dwells in body drops the body down and gets released from it, what does these remain? This, verily, is That.

Death, the central concern of this Upaniṣad, occurs only to individual beings. Every such being is a transient form assumed by the Immortal Self-Substance. What is motal in a being is its visible form and qualities; what remains immortal is its invisible Substance, the qualified. That which perishes is signified by the word *śarīra*. How the *śarīra* contains within it all that perishes, including even the animating principle (*cetanā*) has already been discussed under Verse I.iii.3. In a living being, the Self-Substance is as though confined in a perishable form of the body (*śarīra*). At the disintegration of all that constitutes *śarīra*, on the event of what we term 'death', the Self-Substance will continue to exist, but in an indistinct form, to assume yet another distinct form, to be sure, as the Self cannot exist without some form. What disintegrates is the perishable, visible aspect, the quality aspect, of the Substance. What remains is that Substance alone, symbolized by *AUṀ*.

The releasing of the Self from the body is usually understood as the soul's leaving the physical body at death. In the context of the Vedāntic vision being taught here, it means the Self-Substance becoming free of conditioning factors such as body, sense, mind, animating principle and so on, just as gold, on melting, is freed of the shape of the ornament. Getting rid of identifying oneself with the conditioning factors like body could occur any moment while living. It is what is called enlightenment. It is the Final Liberation experienced by a *jñānin*.

It is this Eternally Free Self Reality — *Atman* — that Naciketas perceives within the mansion!

न प्राणेन नापानेन मर्त्यो जीवति कश्चन ।
इतरेण तु जीवन्ति यस्मिन्नेतावुपाश्रितौ ॥ ५ ॥

na prāṇena nāpānena martyo jīvati kaścana ।
itareṇa tu jīvanti yasminn etāvupāśritau ॥ 5 ॥

Neither by *prāṇa* nor by *apāna* does any mortal whatsoever live; by the other indeed do all live on which these too depend.

In our ignorance we identify ourselves with the body, and not even with all the factors constituting the body, but only with the grossest aspect, and think of ourselves as being kept alive by *prāṇa* and *apāna*. These two which are merely part of the numerous subtle functions of the one

Substance, do not constitute the life-supporting principle. The Self, whereon these two depend and of which the two are aspects of self-expression, is the one all-suporting Substance. Realizing It as his own self, as himself, the wise one experiences the blissfulness of Immortality while living. The ignorant one, on the other hand, identifying himself with *śarīra*, the body, seeing its disintegration as his own disintegration, is terrified of death, and anxious about the state after death.

One reaps as one sows. Sowing the seeds of ignorance, one reaps death and all the uncertainty associated with death. Sowing the seeds of wisdom, one reaps the fruit of immortality, as is made explicit in the next verse.

हन्त त इदं प्रवक्ष्यामि गुह्यं ब्रह्म सनातनम् ।
यथा च मरणं प्राप्य आत्मा भवति गौतम ॥ ६ ॥

hanta ta idaṁ pravakṣyāmi guhyaṁ brahma
sanātanam ।
yathā ca maraṇaṁ prāpya ātmā bhavati gautama ॥ 6 ॥

Come! I shall now declare to you the mystery of *Brahman*, the everlasting; and also how the self continues to exist after death, O Gautama.

Yama has already explained what the meaning content of *AUṀ* is, what *ātman/Brahman* is, how It is the all-pervading eternal Reality, how one's awareness of being one with that Immoratal Reality makes one immortal and liberated. Now Yama tells Naciketas that he intends to declare the mystery of the everlasting *Brahman*. The central teaching of the Upaniṣad, this mystery is the one directly experienced by *jñānin*s (the wise ones) and aimed at by true seekers (*jijñāsu*s), as the very word *upaniṣad* — meaning secret wisdom — suggests. This experiential awareness is marked by one's realizing one's own birthlessness and deathlessness.

Yama also says, that he will declare how the self continues to exist after death. Considering death as real being a sign of ignorance, as we know in the light of what has been learnt so far, this declaration, though pointing directly to the original question, must be understood as meant for those who are either unwilling to or incapable of awakening. A proper understanding of what follows, therefore, presupposes a discrimination between the two sorts of listeners who are being addressed here: the wise and the ignorant. The declaration meant for the true seeker is not within the grasp of the ignorant, and the one meant for the latter of no relevance to the former. The true wisdom meant for seekers and the fill-in-the-blank answer meant for the ignorant are not to be mixed up promiscuously. Considering the latter as part of the real teaching of the Upaniṣad would cloud the original teaching. The latter declaration is made first in one verse, and Yama then proceeds at length to the declaration of the mystery of *Brahman*, forming the whole of the rest of the chapter.

> योनिमन्ये प्रपद्यन्ते शरीत्वाय देहिनः ।
> स्थाणुमन्येऽनुसंयन्ति यथाकर्म यथाश्रुतम् ।। ७ ।।
>
> *yonim anye prapadyante śarīratvāyā dehinaḥ* ।
> *sthāṇum anye'nusamyanti yathā karma*
> *yathā śrutam* ।। 7 ।।
>
> Some embodied approach wombs for re-embodiment; some others go as stationary objects; according as one's deeds, according as one's learning.

The only verse that directly dwells on the problem of the hereafter in this Upaniṣad, it conforms well with the popular Indian notion of reincarnation of souls in accordance with the virtuousness of past deeds. The word *dehinaḥ*, interpreted as 'souls' literally means the 'embodied ones'. Those of meritorious deeds, according to this popular belief, will be reborn as human beings of higher order, and those of vicious deeds as beings of a lower order, perhaps even as plants and inanimate entities. Rooted in ignorance, such beliefs regard birth and death as real, and in sequal rebirth also as real and inevitable. Forming part of phenomenal becoming, and in no way affecting the one Self-Substance, this cyclic nature of life is considered real by the ignorant.

The perceived nature of the world is in accordance with how one perceives it; and one's perception in turn depends on how one thinks of it. One who thinks of the many as real regards birth and death also as real, as they always go with multiplicity, as made clear already in Verse II. i. 11. Taking the cyclic nature of life as real, ignorant of what the Real is, one is destined to live in the world of birth and death. He who, on the other hand, sees one Reality alone in all transformations, the man of wisdom, remains unaffected by their cyclic nature. It is the ignorant who consider birth and death as real and they alone, according to their own perception, are to be reborn. Citations such as this or its like in the Upaniṣads do not indicate acceptance of birth, death or rebirth, as part of the Real. Rather these declarations are to be seen as meant for those who view the unreal as real, those who are under the spell of *avidyā* (ignorance).

There are persons who, even after reading scriptures like the present Upaniṣad with focused attention and examining all available commentaries, still remain unconvinced of their own immortality, and ask, 'What will happen to me after death?' Conditioned as their minds are by the causal chain of events in life, only a story-like depiction of events after death can appeal to them. The *Chāndogya Upaniṣad* portrays such a graphic picture:

> Those who know this and those who, dwelling in forests, practise faith and austerities, go to light, from light to day, from day to the brighter fortnight, from the brighter fortnight to the brighter half year, from the brighter half year to the year, from the year to the sun, from the sun to the moon, from the moon to lightning. There a person who is not a human being meets him and leads him to *Brahman*. This is path of the gods (*devayāna*).
>
> But those who, living in villages, perform sacrifices, undertake works of public utility, and give alms, go to smoke, from smoke to night, from night to the darker fortnight, from the darker fortnight to the darker half year, from the darker half year they do not reach the year.
>
> From the darker half year they go to the world of manes, from the world of manes to space (*ākāśa*), from space to the moon. This is the king Soma. They are food for gods. Them the gods eat.
>
> Having dwelt there till their works are consumed, they return again the same way they came. They reach space, from space

air. Having become air, they become smoke; having become smoke, they become mist;

Having become mist, they become cloud; having become cloud, they fall as rain. Then they are born as rice and barley, herbs and trees, sesamum and seeds. Thence the exit is most difficult; for whoever eats that food and inseminates, they become like unto him.

Those whose conduct here (on earth) has been good, will quickly attain some good birth — birth as a brāhmaṇa, birth as a kṣatriya (ruler class), or birth as a vaiśya (peasant-merchant class). But those whose conduct here has been evil, will quickly attain some evil birth — birth as a dog, birth as a pig, or birth as a *cāṇḍāla* (the out-caste).

(*Chāndogya Upaniṣad*, V.x.1-7)

With their apparent continuity of events, such narrations appeal to the simple mind of the unlearned. In this story, even the departure of a *jñānin* reaching the world of *Brahman*, is as conceived by an *ajñānin*. No scripture intends to teach ignorance, nor to promote taking the unreal in place of the real, and such citations though part of the Upaniṣadic text, are not to be considered part of its teaching proper. Still they do serve the laudable purpose of distinguishing *vidyā* and its effects from *avidyā* and its effects.

Not that this theory, though untestable, is of no value. Its moral impact on the common man has always been immense. It dissuades him from vices, inciting as it does the fear of having to be reborn among the lowest of creatures. Moreover, this theory offers clear hope of attaining liberation (*mukti*) at least in a distant future birth, otherwise seemingly out of reach for the ignorant.

Barring the idea that a particular individual reincarnates as a new individual, the theory that one's *karma* (actions) and the knowledge one acquires, decide one's future is not quite repugnant to the non-dual stance of Vedānta. The one Self-Reality, essentially creative and vital, does not remain inactive. Living as It is, It ever assumes new forms and gives up old ones. Just as the form of a new ornament is determined by the fancying of the goldsmith, how the world should be is fancied by the Self, and It decides what must happen next. What happens next depends on what happens now and on what is fancied and thought of now. The size and force of any breaker depends on the size and force of the previous one; that is to say, the *karma* of one breaker decides the *karma* of the succeeding one. Likewise, every event in nature decides what happens next and how it is to happen.

In a different sense, the *karma* theory conforms with the science of genetics. All one's deeds, the knowledge one acquires and inherits, all instinctive dispositions and personal characteristics, are encoded in one's genes and are transmitted to the next generation. All such inherited factors are covered by the *karma* concept. It is thus the *karma* of one generation that decides the *karma* and nature of the next. In what manner everything in this world is active at this moment decides how the world will be the next moment. Such is the way the Self-Reality unfolds itself as this world of actions. With his volition capable of deciding what to do and what not to do, man's role in deciding the future of the world and the future of the human race is crucial.

One factor distinguishes the *karma* theory from genetics: the question of whether it is the soul or the gene with all the encoded information that transmigrates. The difference is subtle and not of much consequence. The *karma* theory can be viewed as a premitive form of genetics, formulated when science and technology in the modern sense was quite unknown, guided only by the intuitive insights, of the seers' penetrative vision.

The *karma* theory, though formulated and voiced by *ṛṣis* essentially to be of use to the simple minds of the unlearned, has distinct value as a moral force, and as a source of hope. It also helps to understand how the *karma* (action) and knowledge of the present decides the future of mankind and of the world.

(For a more detailed study on the subject see our book *Karma and Reincarnation*).

य एष सुप्तेषु जागर्ति कामं कामं पुरुषे निर्मिमाणः ।
तदेव शुक्रं तद् ब्रह्म तदेवामृतमुच्यते ।
तस्मिँल्लोकाः श्रिताः सर्वे तदु नात्येति कश्चन ।
एतद् वै तत् ॥ ८ ॥

ya eṣa supteṣu jāgarti kāmaṁ kāmaṁ puruṣo ।
nirmimāṇaḥ ।
tad eva śukraṁ tad brahma tad evāmṛtam
ucyate ।
tasmil lokāḥ śritāḥ sarve tad u nātyeti kaścana ।
etad vai tat ॥ 8 ॥

He who is awake even in those asleep, the *puruṣa* who fashions desire after desire out of Himself — He indeed is the Pure; he indeed is *Brahman*; He indeed is called the Immortal. On Him all the worlds do rest; and no one ever goes beyond Him. This verily is That.

What happens to the departed according to the view of those consider death real, was stated in the previous verse. It was seen that a study of the ignorant vision of life is not what is meant to be taught in an Upaniṣad. Now the *ṛṣi* proceeds to declare the mystery of *Brahman*, the real teaching from this verse till the end of the chapter.

Mysteries are inexplicable, and the mystery of *Brahman* is the most enigmatic of all, and this declaration is not really meant for elaboration. Rather is it to be cogitated and meditated on until enlightenment arises.

Being *sat*, *Brahman* exists in everything, as everything and as all the worlds. Being *cit*, It functions as altering states of consciousness between the extremes of deep sleep and complete wakefulness, and is conscious of Its own altering states. It is thus the consciousness that is aware even in one who sleeps. Being *ānanda*, It has the inner urge to unfold Itself as everything enjoyable, as the one who enjoys and as enjoyment.

The desire (*kāma*) for this self-unfoldment is unceasing. Our existence here as individual enjoyers is merely part of the self-unfoldment of the Self, our desire for enjoyment, but a facet of the desire of the Self for self-expression. Overlooking this reality, we treat ourselves as enjoyers and all else as objects to be enjoyed.

When I realize myself, not as an independent individual being, but as a minute element of *sat-cit-ānanda,* I begin to see myself, the Self, as the most transparent (*śukra*) of all realities, as *Brahman*, as Immortal (*amṛta*) — beyond birth, death and rebirth. In the Immortal Self (I), in *Brahman*, do all the worlds, rest. Nothing beyond me is there to be known; nothing beyond *Brahman* is there is to be known. The Reality I was in search of is That. I am That. That is what Naciketas perceived inside the mansion!

अग्निर्यथैको भुवनं प्रविष्टो रूपं रूपं प्रतिरूपो बभूव ।
एकस्तथा सर्वभूतान्तरात्मा रूपं रूपं प्रतिरूपो बहिश्च ॥ ९ ॥

agnir yathaiko bhuvanaṁ praviṣṭo
rūpaṁ rūpaṁ pratirūpo babhūva ।
ekas tathā sarva-bhūtāntarātmā
rūpaṁ rūpaṁ pratirūpo bahiś ca ॥ 9 ॥

As fire, though one, entering the world, assumes forms corresponding to every form, so the One is the inner substance (*antarātmā*) of all things, corresponding in form to every form, and also existing outside them.

वायुर्यथैको भुवनं प्रविष्टो रूपं रूपं प्रतिरूपो बभूव ।
एकस्तथा सर्वभूतान्तरात्मा रूपं रूपं प्रतिरूपो बहिश्च ॥ १० ॥

vāyur yathaiko bhuvanaṁ praviṣṭo
rūpaṁ rūpaṁ pratirūpo babhūva ।
ekas tathā sarva-bhūtāntarātmā
rūpaṁ rūpaṁ pratirūpo bahiś ca ॥ 10 ॥

As air, though one, entering the world assumes forms corresponding to every form, so the One is the inner substance (*antarātmā*) of all things, corresponding in form to every form, and also existing outside them.

The easiest and most direct way to meditate on the mystery of *Brahman* as the all-pervading Substance and the Substance that pervades one's own being, is delineated in these two verses. Not that they are the only ways of meditating; anything in this world can be meditated on as a specific form in which the one expresses Itself.

Fire, though visible only when burning, pervades every visible thing in this universe; any two things rubbed together brings out the latent fire. Where does it hide if not everywhere? Even the ocean is supposedly pervaded by the fire-principle *baḍavāgni*, the reason why oceans do not overflow. Once become visible, its colour, nature of flame, heat and other qualities vary depending on factors like the fuel it is able to consume and the wind force. However, fire in all such various forms remains one.

The invisible *Brahman* too hides everywhere in all visible and imaginable forms. Fire pervades only within things, but *Brahman* pervades within as well as without. Indeed even the appearance of within and without are due to the pervasiveness of *Brahman*, as both within and without are cognized in consciousness or *cit*. The seeker therefore has to meditate on *Brahman* as pervading within and without his own being.

So too is the extensiveness of air. Having no form of its own, within a pot it assumes the form of the pot; within a house it assumes the house-form. The Self, likewise, though formless as such, assumes my form, your form, every form. What is outside you and me is also none other than *Brahman*. *Brahman* alone having existence of its own, all existence, within and without, are derived of It.

To liken *Brahman* to fire, while meditating on Its burning urge for self-expression, and likening it to air when meditating on Its limitless extensiveness, are common among *ṛṣis*. The former analogy reveals the vertical creativity of *Brahman* like that of Śiva, and the latter Its horizontal creativity, like that of *śakti*. Real non-dual creativity could well be subjected to such analysis, as an aid to transcend such dualities in one's own contemplative insight, where the meditator-meditated duality also evaporates.

All the forms Immortal *Brahman* assumes are evanescent. The meditator, one such form, must therefore meditate on the Immortal *Brahman*, as the Substance which pervades, and has become his own evanescent form which constitutes both the physical and mental aspects.

सूर्यो यथा सर्वलोकस्य चक्षु-
र्न लिप्यते चाक्षुषैर्बाह्यदोषैः ।
एकस्तथा सर्वभूतान्तरात्मा
न लिप्यते लोकदुःखेन बाह्यः ।। ११ ।।

sūryo yathā sarva lokasya cakṣur
na lipyate cākṣuṣair bāhya doṣaiḥ ।
ekas tathā sarva-bhūt āntarātmā
na lipyate loka-duḥkhena bāhyaḥ ॥ 11 ॥

As the Sun, the eye of the whole world, is not defiled by the external defects of eyes, so the inner Substance of all beings, transcendental as it is, is untainted by the sorrows of the world.

Our eyes, in sunlight, see the world partly, the whole world seen only by the sun in its own light. The sun thus is the eye of the world. Yet the perceived brighteness of the sun and the perceived nature of the world depend on the condition of the perceiving eye and mind. The colours perceived depend the degree and variation of colour-blindness, while the size and clarity of the object depend on the degree of short or long-sight. Similar is the role of the perceiver's mind especially in regard to responses to what is perceived. Everyone perhaps has defective eye-sight to some degree and none possibly knows what the object actually looks like. These defects, however, in no way touch either the all-illumining sun, the eye of the world, or the real but unknown nature of the object.

Our perception of life is also tainted by preconceptions of life as an ocean of sorrows. But for all our wrong conception of life, the untainted transparency of *Brahman* remains unaffected. What one needs to realizing It, is to wash off the grime — of ignorance concerning oneself and to give up one's identity with external appearances. Then will one see, instead of misery, sorrow and evil, only *sat-cit-ānanda*.

एको वशी सर्वभूतान्तरात्मा
एकं रूपं बहुधा यः करोति ।
तमात्मस्थं येऽनुपश्यन्ति धीरा-
स्तेषां सुखं शाश्वतं नेतरेषाम् ॥ १२ ॥

eko vaśī sarva-bhūtāntarātmā
ekaṁ rūpaṁ bahudhā yaḥ karoti ।
tam ātmasthaṁ ye'nupaśyanti dhīrās-
teṣāṁ sukhaṁ śāśvataṁ netareṣām ॥ 12 ॥

The one inner restrainer, the one inner Substance of all that has come into being, the one who makes Himself manifold in form — the wise who constantly perceive Him as abiding in themselves, alone, and no others, have eternal Happiness.

The Substance that underlies appearances is called 'being' in Western philosophy, and everything that emerges of 'being' is called 'becoming'; the equivalent Indian terms are *sat* and *bhāva*. That which has already emerged from 'being' is *bhūta*. It is the one Substance, the *sat*, the being, that withholds within it all potential for the emanation of *bhūtas*. The same Substance sends forth *bhūtas* from Itself and appears as the world. While appearing so, all multitudinous forms continue to be of the selfsame Substance. As abiding in each and every *bhūta*, the Substance is called *bhūta-antarātmā* (*bhūta* + *antar* + *ātmā*), *antar* meaning 'within'.

One who knows this secret sees *Brahman* in his own being, in activities, in problems, and in their solution. Seeing only *Brahman* in all aspects of life, makes life peaceful and joyful in spite of the vagaries and problems of day-to-day affairs. Seeing death as one such vagary, the wise one finds himself immortal. One thus enlightened brings enlightenment to others and such a person of firmness is called *dhīra*.

नित्योऽनित्यानां चेतनश्चेतनाना-
मेको बहूनां यो विदधाति कामान् ।
तमात्मस्थं येऽनुपश्यन्ति धीरा-
स्तेषां शान्तिः शाश्वती नेतरेषाम् ।। १३ ।।

nityo'nityānāṁ cetanaś cetanānām
eko bahūnāṁ yo vidadhāti kāmān ।
tamātmasthaṁ ye'nupaśyanti dhīrās-
teṣāṁ śāntiḥ śāśvatī netareṣām ।। 13 ।।

The everlasting in all that is ephemeral, the consciousness in all that is conscious, the one in all the many, the dispenser of all desires — the wise who constantly perceive Him as abiding in themselves, alone, and no others, have eternal Peace.

One eternal water abides in all transient wave forms; one eternal gold abides in all transient ornaments; even so one eternal *Brahman* abides in all the transience of the world. *Sat* (Existence) in essence, It is the everlasting in all that is ephemeral; *cit* (Consciousness) in essence, It is the one consciousnes in all that is conscious. (The supposedly inert physical factors are also none other than gross manifestation of the same *cit*.) The One attributeless causal Substance, It is the one in the many with attributes. The arousal of desires in beings, their corresponding fulfilments and through them ensuring the onward flow of life, are all ordained and dispensed by *Brahman* alone. Each person, seeing himself in the place of a wave, in the place of an ornament, realizes himself to be the one Immortal Reality that assumes fleeting attributes. He alone finds Peace in life. This is the Peace that Naciketas experienced within the heart of the Mansion of Reality!

तदेतदिति मन्यन्तेऽनिर्देश्यं परमं सुखम् ।
कथं नु तद्विजानीयां किमु भाति विभाति वा ।। १४ ।।

tad etad iti manyante'nirdeśyaṁ paramaṁ sukham ।
kathaṁ nu tad vijānīyāṁ kimu bhāti vibhāti vā ।। 14 ।।

'That is it !' Thus they get enlightened of the Supreme Happiness, the inexpressible. How, now, should I know That? Does it shine as it is? Or, does It shine in specific forms?

The meditation pursued so far from Verse 8 onwards of this chapter, supported by all the preceding philosophical speculations, leads the seeker to the fully enlightened feelings of 'That is it !' No enlightened Guru is able to show this enlightenment to another, not even to the most intimate disciple. Nor can an orator describe it to his listeners. The question then arises: How should, then one know That? Is It to be understood as a pure effulgence that shines as it is? Or, does It shine specifically in, through, and as each of our experiences?

The next verse, concluding the chapter, answers this question of Naciketas.

न तत्र सूर्यो भाति न चन्द्रतारकं
नेमा विद्युतो भान्ति कुतोऽयमग्निः ।
तमेव भान्तमनुभाति सर्वं
तस्य भासा सर्वमिदं विभाति ।। १५ ।।

na tatra sūryo bhāti na candra-tārakaṁ
n'emā vidyuto bhānti kuto'yamagniḥ ।
tameva bhāntam anubhāti sarvaṁ
tasya bhāsā sarvam idaṁ vibhāti ।। 15 ।।

The Sun illumines it not, nor the moon and stars. Nor do these lightning-flashes illumine It; let alone this fire. Everything shines because of Its shining; all these individually shine as illumined by That.

The illumining factors in our ordinary experience of seeing things distinctly are the sun, the moon, stars and fire, but none of these luminaries can illuminate *Brahman*. All of them form part of the cosmic system, which is the self-expresssion of *Brahman*. Their capability to shine and illumine is also ordained by *Brahman*, and therefore their luminosity cannot illumine *Brahman*. On the other hand, they shine because of the self-effulgence of *Brahman*.

The enquiring mind, itself illumined by *Brahman*, is here desirous of knowing *Brahman*. Though capable of clearly understanding all other things, mind is incapable of knowing *Brahman*, its own source and illuminator. What the mind can do is only to realize: 'I am merely a tiny speck of that great fire; I do not exist apart from it; I am That.'

The problem, of how to communicate the incommunicable, how to know the unknowable, is of an epistemological order, but the answer given is more of an ontological nature, relating to the self-effulgent causal substance. The answer might thus seem beside the point. Seeing *sat* (ontological existence) as *cit* (epistemological consciousness) is what brings the answer right to the point. *Sat* being *cit* in essence, the transformations in the *sat* aspect are in effect transformations in the *cit* aspect too. Like in a trepeze act, Indian seers explain the inexplicable by elucidating the *sat* aspect in terms of *cit* and *vice versa*, where letting go off one necessitates grasping the other. Only intense cogitation, reinforced by meditation, preferably with the guidance of an enlightened Guru, can help disentangle this conundrum. Similar is the way *ānanda* is related to *sat* and *cit*.

The next chapter goes deeper into this problem and the mystery of *Brahman*.

Chapter III

तृतीया वल्ली

ऊर्ध्वमूलोऽवाक्शाख एषोऽश्वत्थः सनातनः ।
तदेव शुक्रं तद् ब्रह्म तदेवामृतमुच्यते ।
तस्मिल्लोकाः श्रिताः सर्वे तदु नात्येति कश्चन ।
एतद् वै तत् ।। १ ।।

ūrdhva-mulo'vāk śakha eṣo'śvattaḥ sanātanaḥ ।
tad eva śukraṁ tad brahma tad evāmṛtam ucyate ।
tasmil lokāḥ śritāḥ sarve tadu n ātyeti kaścana ।
etad vai tat ।। 1 ।।

Rooted above with branches downwards is this eternal fig-tree. That indeed is the Pure; that indeed is *Brahman*. That indeed is called the Immortal. On It are hung all the worlds. No one goes beyond It. This verily is That.

THIS chapter, which continues to dwell on the mystery of *Brahman*, going deeper into the epistemological-ontological riddle, leads to the conclusive stance of Vedānta, an all-inclusive vision of the world, a sweeping vision of life. Problems such as that of death, assume enormous proportions in life when considered as belonging to the individual. However, visualized as pertaining to the overall scheme of life, the same problems lose their fearsome enormity and are felt as giving perfection to the overall flow of life. Leading us to such a vision is the attempt of all scriptures, like the present Upaniṣad.

Without much thought we visualize and plan our life, taking into account only whatever is directly visible. Only when faced with problems, do we start to think seriously and then we discover that many of its essential factors, like the roots of a tree, are hidden from us. Roots, the nourishing and stabilizing part of the tree, remain always hidden beneath the earth. Likewise in the tree of life, its most basic factor always remains hidden. The deeper we go into the basics, the vaguer and more mysterious it appears. It is not however in dark nether regions as of the earth that these are rooted. Most subtle, most sublime, they are rooted in the higher realms of knowledge. The visible part of this tree grows downwards becoming more earthly as it grows more detailed. This tree of life is eternal. The birth and death of individual beings are nothing but the budding of new leaves and the falling off of old ones, part of the eternal progression of life. The visible part of this tree cannot and does not remain without the invisible. The visible part, what we call the world, depends on the invisible part, just as ornaments depend on the gold for their appearance. One is meaningless and impossible without the other. This indivisible Reality, the non-dual Reality, is *Brahman*, the Pure, the Immortal. Nothing is to be known beyond That. Knowing It, the essence of everything, in fact means knowing everything. Knowing It, one finds oneself a speck of It, with everything visible as well as invisible contained within. Seeing thus the secret of the here and the hereafter within oneself, one remains self-satisfied. Seeing oneself one with *Brahman*, one's problems vanish into the problemless *Brahman*. One thus simply remains peaceful in oneself, in That Self, in *Brahman* the Immortal.

The *Bhagavad Gītā* uses the same fig-tree analogy in its Chapter XV. What is likened in the *Gītā* to the upside-down fig-tree is the *puruṣa* or knowledge aspect of self-existence symbolically represented by the Vedas, in their capacity as the manifest form of knowledge. The *Gītā* directs that the fig-tree be cut down mercilessly with the weapon of detachment in order to attain the supreme, whereas the fig-tree of the *Kaṭha Upaniṣad* is meant to be understood and realized by one as the Immortal living Reality in oneself.

यदिदं किञ्च जगत् सर्वं प्राण एजति निःसृतम् ।
महद्भयं वज्रमुद्यतं य एतद् विदुरमृतास्ते भवन्ति ।। २ ।।

yad idaṁ kiñca jagat sarvaṁ prāṇa ejati niḥsṛtam ।
mahad bhayaṁ vajram udyataṁ ya etad vidur
amṛtās te bhavanti ॥ 2 ॥

Whatever there is as this changeful world, had emerged from and moves within this *prāṇa*, the great awesome, upraised- thunder- bolt-like. Knowing It one becomes immortal.

भयादस्याग्निस्तपति भयात्तपति सूर्यः ।
भयादिन्द्रश्च वायुश्च मृत्युर्धावति पञ्चमः ॥ ३ ॥

bhayād asyāgnis tapati bhayāt tapati sūryaḥ ।
bhayād indraś ca vāyuśca mṛtyur dhāvati
pañcamaḥ ॥ 3 ॥

Afraid of Him fire (*Agni*) does burn; afraid of Him the sun (*Sūrya*) does give out heat; afraid of Him *Indra* and *Vāyu* (wind) do their jobs; afraid of Him Death, the fifth, does speed along.

The ultimate goal of Vedānta is the seeker's attaining final liberation from all sufferings and bondages. This liberation is what is known as *mokṣa* or *mukti*. Acquiring well defined knowledge of what is Real is not so important as the attainment of this goal. Vedānta in that sense is a value-based philosophy, and to that extent pragmatic. The Real, the greatest of all mysteries, is neither definable nor understandable. Our life and its problems are all fleeting specks of that great, mysterious fire. This understanding alleviates the sorrows and problems of life. A shift from the search for the Real, to the attainment of Immortality as such and as freedom from sorrows, is therefore placed at the close of almost all Vedāntic scriptures, the present Upaniṣad no exception.

One mysterious *Brahman* unfolds itself as everything, as all the worlds. Helpless though we are, in spite of all our volition, our life too is part of it. This awareness reduces all our burdens to nothing. Burdens, if any, then are *Brahman*'s, not ours. Along with this liberation becomes ours the immortality of *Brahman*.

The unfolding of immutable *Brahman* as this mutable world, has a functional system of its own. Only complying with that system can any entity move and have its being. The sun, for example, cannot one day think of rising in the west. The moon is incapable of shining at day time, even if it so desires. Fire cannot burn downwards and air cannot remain motionless. We, in our evanescent body, should not expect to live for ever; the body has to perish, and it is the function of Death to bring this about.

When an individual entity in this overall system feels that it has an independent way of existing and functioning, then the same mysterious *Brahman* is felt to be awesome, to be feared and respected, something unapproachable whose command cannot be defied, like a thunderbolt unleashed.

Man is distinct from all other beings because of his free will. Man alone and no other being feels this unease. Its only solution is: to subjugate your free will to that of *Brahman* or God; to mould your own will so that it becomes one with the will of God, thus actualizing the oneness of the existence of God and yours.

Brahman, mysteriously brimming with life, is here given the epithet *prāṇa*, not as mere organic vitality, but, more true to the literal sense of the word, as that reality which lives and enlivens. The word *prāṇa*, is derived from the root *an*, meaning, to be alive (*an prāṇane*).

इह चेदशकद् बोद्धुं प्राक् शरीरस्य विस्रसः ।
ततः सर्गेषु लोकेषु शरीरत्वाय कल्पते ।। ४ ।।

iha ced aśakad boddhuṁ prāk śarīrasya visrasaḥ ।
tataḥ sargeṣu lokeṣu śarīratvāya kalpate ।। 4 ।।

This (wisdom) become convinced of here and now, before the dissolution of the body, one is fit to become incarnate as all the worlds.

यथादर्शे तथात्मनि
यथा स्वप्ने तथा पितृलोके ।
यथाप्सु परीव ददृशे तथा गन्धर्वलोके
छायातपयोरिव ब्रह्मलोके ।। ५ ।।

yathādarśe tathātmani
yathā svapne tathā pitṛloke ।
yathāpsu parīva dadṛśe tathā gandharva-loke
chāyātapayor iva brahma-loke ।। 5 ।।

As in a mirror, so is seen in oneself;
as in dream, so is seen the world of manes;
as in water, so is seen the world of Gandharvas around,
as light and shadow, so is seen the world of *Brahman*.

A gold ornament, on realizing 'I am gold', forgoes its ornament identity and attains the identity of gold. With that vision the ornament looks around at other ornaments, and sees itself embodied as all of them. Knowing oneself as *Brahman*, likewise, enables the knower to see all the worlds as his own embodied form. He sees himself mirrored in the world. As the *Īśa Upaniṣad* puts it, he sees himself in all beings and all beings in himself. This realization is to be accomplished while living in this world, before the dissolution of the body. Liberation attainable only after the dissolution of the body, a state known to none, is meaningless. Advancing still another stept the *Kena Upaniṣad* says, not realizing it while living in this world is a great loss indeed (Verse14).

Things in the mineral kingdom are incapable of comprehending how the animal and vegetable kingdoms thrive. Beings of the animal kingdom are incapable of appreciating human life. Human beings, likewise, are not capable of knowing the way of the higher worlds. Man's incapacity to know something cannot be accepted as a criterion to maintain its non-existence. So too in the case of the existence of other worlds. The ancient *ṛṣi*s, therefore, instead of denying the possibility of other worlds, poetically conceived of many such: the world of gods (*devaloka*), the world of the departed souls (*pitṛ-loka*), the world of Gandharvas, among them.

The most clear and distinct world one directly perceives is that of his own self-existence. The knower of the Self sees the entire world mirrored in himself, and he mirrored in the world.

The *pitṛloka* (the world of manes) is where departed souls supposedly remain till the time of their return to this world. Though the reality of such worlds is like that of dream, our mind is easily drawn to imagining such things and they are therefore not to be ruled out, just as dreams cannot be ruled out. Only, one who knows the Self, will understand it to be a dream-world.

Gandharvas are mythological demi-gods, the guardians of fire-arts. More blurred is the vision of their world, comparable to images in water.

Brahma-loka, as the ignorant conceive it, is the world where the departed souls of *jñānins* (men of wisdom) go never to return. In a *jñānin*'s view, however, all the worlds are *Brahman* embodied and therefore constitute *Brahma-loka* (the world of *Brahman*). *Brahman* does not exist without embodying itself as the worlds, the two related as light and shadow, one meaningless without the other.

इन्द्रियाणां पृथग्भावमुदयास्तमयौ च यत् ।
पृथगुत्पद्यमानानां मत्वा धीरो न शोचति ॥ ६ ॥

indriyāṇāṁ pṛthag-bhāvam udayāstamayau ca yat ।
pṛthak utpadyamānānāṁ matvā dhīro na śocati ॥ 6 ॥

The senses, one different from the other, emanate (from Him). The wise and firm one who knows their state of being so, and how do they emerge and remerge, he sorrows not.

So far it has been elucidated, how one attains the final goal by knowing that all the heavenly luminaries and all the worlds have their origin and existence in *Brahman*. From this verse onwards is being shown how, by knowing that the individuating factors in us had also their origin and existence in *Brahman*, one attains the final goal.

Senses are the doors through which consciousness comes out to get in contact with the world. Senses again are the doorway for all worldly objects to enter our consciousness. A door opening both ways, in and out, senses are the most evident but very subtle individuating factor in human beings. They are so structured that each of the five senses comes in contact with the distinguishing quality of each of the five gross elements of the cosmic system: nose contacts with smell, the quality of earth; tongue with taste, the quality of water; eyes with form, the quality of fire; skin with touch, the quality of air; and ears with sound, the quality of space. The structure and function of senses are so integrally related to the cosmic system that the two are inseparable. Yet each sense is distinct as is each quality sensed, and each object perceived also is distinct. It is one Mysteriously Conscious Reality—*Brahman* — that unalterably systematized all these subtle factors. Or, it is the self-unfoldment of *Brahman* that assumes the form of this functionally perfect system.

Each person, while percieving and enjoying objects with his senses, has to enquire into its working. As this enquiry reaches intensity, he finds the one Conscious Reality that is behind all these, and his own oneness with that Immortal Reality, and finally his own immortality.

How this search for the reality behind sense perception leads one finally to the one Immortal Reality is elucidated methodically in the next two verses.

इन्द्रियेभ्यः परं मनो मनसः सत्त्वमुत्तमम् ।
सत्त्वादधि महानात्मा महतोऽव्यक्तमुत्तमम् ।। ७ ।।

indriyebhyaḥ paraṁ mano manasaḥ sattvam uttamam ।
sattvād adhi mahān ātmā mahato'vyaktam uttamam ।। 7 ।।

Beyond senses is mind; above mind is pure being; over pure being is the great self; above the great is the unmanifest.

अव्यक्तात् तु परः पुरुषो व्यापकोऽलिङ्ग एव च ।
यं ज्ञात्वा मुच्यते जन्तुरमृतत्वं च गच्छति ।। ८ ।।

avyaktāt tu paraḥ puruṣo vyāpako'liṅga eva ca ।
yaṁ jñātvā mucyate jantur amṛtatvaṁ ca gacchati ।। 8 ।।

Still beyond the unmanifest is *puruṣa*, the all-pervading with no distinguishing mark. Knowing Him, any living being gets liberated and attains immortality.

Though following the same order of interiorization of search adopted in Verses 10 and 11 of Chapter III of Part I, unlike in that context, the emphasis here is on experiencial awareness of the goal already attained, whereas the former context was that of indicating the goal yet to be attained. Delving deeper and deeper into one's own being is perceived experientially the indwelling *puruṣa* (person), beyond which no interiorization is possible. *Puruṣa*, we know, is the dweller in the city, but the city He dwells in, as now experienced, is not merely the individual body, but is all the worlds.

Description in the two contexts varies only in one slight detail: *buddhi* (intelligence, awareness) of the former is designated as *sattvam* (pure being) in the latter, but both in essence convey the same sense. The *mahān* (the great) of both the contexts has *ātmā* appended to it, though each step in this gradation in fact could be conceived as a different version of *ātmā* (the Self), each conditioned in a different way by a different attribute and having a different function, whilst the unconditioned *ātmā* is *puruṣa* alone, where even the conditioning of becoming an individuated consciousness is forgone.

The all-pervading unconditioned *puruṣa* has no need of being distinguished from anything; and hence needs no distinguishing mark and so has none. He is thus *aliṅga* (the one that has no distinguishing mark). Experiencing the unconditioned *puruṣa* within and without, one feels, 'I am all-pervading; I am liberated; I am Immortal.'

The ultimate benefit of attaining this transcendental wisdom is two-faced: one, the intuitive apperception of having been liberated, and two, of having attained immortality. This liberation is from self-identity with the body, as well as from the fear of having to die. What is attained is immortality, the one state we all aspire to. To be free from death and to attain immortality, are not two, in essence, both indicate the same non-dual apperception, which is neither the one nor the other in content.

न सन्दृशे तिष्ठति रूपमस्य
न चक्षुषा पश्यति कश्चनैनम् ।
हृदा मनीषा मनसाभिक्लृप्तो
य एतद् विदुरमृतास्ते भवन्ति ।। ९ ।।

na sandṛśe tiṣṭhati rūpam asya
na cakṣuṣā paśyati kaścanainaṁ ।
hṛdā manīṣā manas ābhikḷpto
ya etad vidur amṛtās te bhavanti ॥ 9 ॥

Not within the range of vision, His form is visible to the eyes of none. He is revealed to the vividity of intuitive apperception as the controlling heart of all mental functions. The knowers of Him become immortal.

यदा पञ्चावतिष्ठन्ते ज्ञानानि मनसा सह ।
बुद्धिश्च न विचेष्टति तामाहुः परमां गतिम् ॥ १० ॥

yadā pañcāvatiṣṭhante jñānāni manasā saha ।
buddhiś ca na viceṣṭati tām āhuḥ paramāṁ gatim ॥ 10 ॥

When and where the five (sense) perceptions hold back along with mind, where intellect stirs not, That is said to be the highest attainment.

The world capable of being known is such that each entity in it has a distinguishing mark of its own. *Puruṣa*, the core substance that unfolds itself as the known, the knower and knowledge, has no such distinguishing marks. Senses and mind perform their function of distinguishing one object form another, with the distinguishing marks as the basis for differentiating objects. He having no distinguishing marks, the senses and mind, faced with the need to perceive Him, stand aghast, unable to grasp Him. With nothing existing apart from Him, He needs no distuguishing mark either.

Mind and senses are functional expressions of consciousness, while being also the outlets of the functions of consciousness. The one Unconditioned Consciousness that finds expression thus, in the capacity of its being their controller, is called *manīṭ*, meaning the controlling core, which is none other than *puruṣa* himself. As the central principle that regulates one's own existence and function, the same is sometimes conceived as *hṛt* (heart). All these fit into an apperception of the transparency and vividness of one's own being, all indicated by the usage *manasābhikḷptaḥ* (intuitively perceived vividity) of Verse 9.

Engrossed as we are in the world of the perceivable and the conceivable which are changeful and apparent, subject to birth and death, death and its appendages become matters of great concern. Our concern with *puruṣa*, on the other hand, and our identifying ourselves with that *puruṣa*, not only makes the problem of death vanish by itself, but we find ourselves to have attained immortality. What was visualized by the *ṛṣi* in these lines is therefore to be brought to transparency of vision by intense cogitation and meditation. Similar passages from other Upaniṣads, like the five verses beginning with the one given below of the *Kena Upaniṣad*, also can be kept in mind:

> That which is not thought of by mind,
> But that which is said to think of mind;
> That indeed is *Brahman*;
> Not anything adored here as 'this'.

तां योगमिति मन्यन्ते स्थिरामिन्द्रियधारणाम् ।
अप्रमत्तस्तदा भवति योगो हि प्रभवाप्ययौ ।। ११।।

tāṁ yogam iti manyante sthirām indriyadhāraṇām ।
apramattas tadā bhavati yogo hi prabhav-
āpyayau ।। 11 ।।

> That constant holding back of
> senses is considered yoga, and
> unerring thus one becomes.
> Emergence and remerger
> indeed also constitute yoga.

Senses and mind, by nature, search for their objects outside. Unable as they are to grasp and think of *Brahman*, they, when one is intent on knowing *Brahman*, have determinedly to be restrained from their tendency to turn outwards. Withholding them means letting them remain one with their source, the primeval Consciousness, *Brahman*, instead of going around in search of something else. This restraint results in their merger with *Brahman*, this being the state of yoga in the Vedānta context. Senses and mind thus find their own base, as suggested by the word *dhāraṇā*, meaning finding one's own basic support. Once this support is found, they begin to function in a new way: as various manifestations of one basic Consciousness, where emergence of new functional facets and their remerger are normal. All sense experiences and mental functions would then be perceived as having existence only in the one non-dual Consciousness. This inseparable oneness is a state of yoga. So too are the objects perceived, emerging from and remerging into the one causal Substance inseparable from the Substance; a state of yoga again. This causal Substance is nothing but *Brahman*, non-dual Consciousness in essence.

It is when meandering with no firm basis that the possibility of error arises leading one eventually to repentance. Finding only pure Consciousness — *Brahman* — as one's firm basis and finding all one's activities as taking place within *Brahman* and as part of the self-unfoldment of *Brahman*, one finds oneself the same as *Brahman* in all respects — this being the state of yoga. Beyond good and evil, right and wrong, *Brahman*'s activities would always be unerring (*apramattaḥ*) in nature; the activities of one in the state of yoga would also necessarily be unerring.

It would be improper at the close of an Upaniṣad where the final goal rather than its means is focused on, to consider yoga merely as a spiritual discipline or a means of attainment. As a spiritual discipline it could appropriately have been discussed at the end of the first half of the Upaniṣad. The yoga understood here therefore is evidently the unitive state attained and not the means of attaining. How incomparable and ineffable this yoga state is, we will see in the next verse.

नैव वाचा न मनसा प्राप्तुं शक्यो न चक्षुषा ।
अस्तीति ब्रुवतोऽन्यत्र कथं तदुपलभ्यते ।। १२ ।।

naiva vācā na manasā prāptuṁ śakyo na cakṣuṣā ।
astīti bruvato'nyatra kathaṁ tad upalabhyate ।। 12 ।।

Attainable neither through speech nor through mind nor through eyes is It. Apart from the one who utters, 'It is what exists' how is It obtainable !

अस्तीत्येवोपलब्धव्यस्तत्त्वभावेन चोभयोः ।
अस्तीत्येवोपलब्धस्य तत्त्वभावः प्रसीदति ।। १३ ।।

astītyevopalabdhavyas tattva-bhāvena cobhayoḥ ।
astītyevopalabdhasya tattva-bhāvaḥ prasīdati ।। 13 ।।

Realizable is It as, 'It is what exists', and also as 'the basic Truth'. Of the two, to the one who has realized in the former way the latter becomes revealed of its own.

Words convey the ideas conceived, mind conceives ideas and fancies; senses grasp objects, forming the basis for all conceptualization and fancying; all forming part of my own existence as a living, knowing, and enjoying entity. I myself derive my existence from the One, which is Existence, Consciousness and Value-sensing, all in one: *Brahman*. This causal Reality, the original source of words also, is not confined within any word as its meaning. Neither is It conceivable by mind as one of its objects, nor is It perceived by senses. Word, on the other hand, must realize,'I am derived from that Existence', so also must mind and senses. The one possessing mind and senses, I, also must realize, 'I derive my existence, from that Existence. I do not exist apart from It.' However, in the usual course, unless one is a born seer, this realization does not occur on its own. A Guru who has realized his non-difference from the one Existence has to reveal it, through such words as, 'It is what exists', or better through a silence surcharged with the ecstatic meaning of Oneness. Such silence is the last word of instruction a Guru can give; such cryptical words or silence is the overflow of their mystical ecstacy. The seeker has to enter that flow and become bathed and imbued with the mystical experience thus: 'It is what exists; I am That.' Apart from having this secret imparted to one by a realized Guru, there is no alternative means of attaining the goal, unless one is a born seer.

One's realizing, 'It is what exists' and 'I am That' forms the two terminal steps in the attainment of one's goal, the former an understanding and the latter a mystical ecstacy, suggested by the word *tattva-bhāva* (the state of being That), which even goes to the extent of what is sometimes called 'God intoxication'. To the one who is bathed in the outflow of mystical ecstacy, the Guru saying, 'It is what exists' is enough to move into mystical ecstacy without any further effort, and without any further instruction from the Guru, he realizes, 'I am That' — the final blissfulness and the final grace (*prasāda*) of the Guru.

यदा सर्वे प्रमुच्यन्ते कामा येऽस्य हृदि श्रिताः ।
अथ मर्त्योऽमृतो भवत्यत्र ब्रह्म समश्नुते ।। १४ ।।

yadā sarve pramucyante kāmā ye'sya hṛdi śritāḥ ।
atha martyo'mṛto bhavaty atra brahma
sam aśnute ॥ 14 ॥

A mortal, with all the desires lodged in his heart having fallen off, becomes immortal and enjoys *Brahman*'s intimacy as well.

यदा सर्वे प्रभिद्यन्ते हृदयस्येह ग्रन्थयः ।
अथ मर्त्योऽमृतो भवत्येतावद्ध्यनुशासनम् ॥ १५ ॥

yadā sarve prabhidyante hṛdayasyeha granthayaḥ ।
atha martyo'mṛto bhavati etāvaddhy
anuśāsanam ॥ 15 ॥

A mortal, with all the knots of the heart having cut off here and now, becomes immortal. Thus far indeed is the wisdom teaching.

The expectation of enjoying an object makes it dear to us. This expectation arises from the notion that our identity is with body and that the objects in our possession can make us happy. Attaining the clarity of vision that all happiness has its source within ourselves, not in objects, we find ourselves free of all desires. All objects, and the world of which they form a part, have no existence apart from the Self, apart from oneself. Realizing this, rid of all false personal identities, one is free of all personal desires. Losing one's personal identity means gaining identity with *Brahman*, a state of intimacy with *Brahman*. Changing on to personal identity, one thinks of oneself as mortal and feels destined to die. Free from the identification with the body, what is gained is oneness with the immortal *Brahman*, thus oneself becoming immortal.

To think of oneself as so and so is a knot knit by oneself in one's own heart (*hṛt*), the focal point of one's personal identity. To think that fulfilling such and such a desire would make one's life meaningful is another knot. The idea that the dissolution of body marks the extinction of self-existence is yet another not of ignorance. Realizing oneness with *Brahman*, realizing the Self, makes one free of all knots, wisdom being the one blade that cuts through all knots in a single stroke. Wisdom thus frees one from the notion of being a mortal; it makes one immortal. Questions of death and the state after, do not arise then to torment one any more.

Thus far is the wisdom teaching of this Upaniṣad; the attainment of Immortality marks the culmination of wisdom. One is then filled with the self-contentment of knowing that nothing more there is to gain in life.

शतं चैका च हृदयस्य नाड्य-
स्तासां मूर्धानमभिनिःसृतैका।
तयोर्ध्वमायन्नमृतत्वमेति
विष्वङ्ङन्या उत्क्रमणे भवन्ति ।। १६ ।।

satam caikā ca hṛdayasya nāḍyas-
tāsāṁ mūrdhānam abhiniḥsṛtaikā ।
tayordhvam āyann amṛtatvam eti
viṣvaṅṅ anyā utkramaṇe bhavanti ।। 16 ।।

One hundred and one are the channels of the heart. Of them, one flows right up to the crown of the head. Pursuing it, is attained immortality. Dissipated as they are, the others are the cause of death.

अङ्गुष्ठमात्रः पुरुषोऽन्तरात्मा
सदा जनानां हृदये सन्निविष्टः ।
तं स्वाच्छरीरात् प्रवृहेन्मुञ्जादिवेषीकां धैर्येण
तं विद्याच्छुक्रममृतं तं विद्याच्छुक्रममृतमिति ।। १७ ।।

aṅguṣṭha mātraḥ puruṣo'ntarātmā
sadā janānāṁ hṛdaye sanniviṣṭaḥ ।
taṁ svāccharīrāt pravṛhen muñjād iveṣīkāṁ dhairyeṇa
taṁ vidyāt śukram amṛtaṁ
taṁ vidyāt śukram amṛtam iti ।। 17 ।।

That *puruṣa* of the measure of a thumb, the innermost Self, is ever seated in the heart of beings. He is to be uplifted with unerring firmness from one's own perishable aspects, like an arrow-shaft out from a reed.

Know Him as the Pure, the Immortal. Know Him as the Pure, the Immortal.

Since the teaching proper reached its finale at the last verse, as made explicit there, these two verses, seemingly out of place, appear to dilute and disturb the serene conclusion of the Upaniṣad. For this reason, some scholars think they are later interpolations.

The psychological heart and its knots, of the last verse, are metaphorically conceived here as the physiological heart and the numerous arteries that branch out. Severing these knots makes clear the one path of wisdom that leads to immortality. Likewise, from the physiological heart are also spread out, arteries, hundreds in number, all leading to horizontal diversification, far from leading to unitiveness. Yet one channel, though imaginary, goes to the crown of the head symbolizing the vertical ascent of the contemplative mind to unity and finally to immortality. It is the distinction between the two paths of knowing unitively and knowing multifariously that are symbolized in this otherwise physiological picture. This archaic concept of the Upaniṣad *r̥ṣi*, was revised by the modern *r̥ṣi* Narayana Guru in his *Ātmopadeśa Śatakam* (One Hundred Verses of Self-Instruction). The infinite potential of consciousness could, according to him, be classified in two: *anya* (the other) and *sama* (the same); the former he defined as seeing the many as many and the latter as knowing all experiences as one consciousness expressing itself in different ways (see Verses 36 to 42). The former leads to the awareness of multiplicity and eventual miseries, and the latter to non-dual awareness and immortality.

A popular Indian belief holds that if soul leaves the body through the horizontally spread out channels, it is destined to be reborn, whereas, if it leaves through the one upward channel, it will reach the world of *Brahman*. The *r̥ṣi* of the Upaniṣad, or the interpolator as the case may be, gives the belief a new colouring in sense, and made use of the concept to discriminate the paths of wisdom and ignorance.

Another Indian concept, especially among those who practise meditation, considers that *ātmā*, of the size of thumb and of the form of a non-flickering flame, is located at the middle of one's heart. This concept also is made use of in distinguishing the two paths. To differentiate the body (*śarīra*) and Self (*ātman*) aspects of our existence and to choose the unitive path of the Self, requires an unrelenting and inexorable firmness on the part of the seeker, comparable to the determined search of a skilled archer for the arrow-shafts among wild reeds. The *śarīra* (body) symbolized by the wild reeds consists of all the perishable aspects of our existence including the animating principle. To extricate the imperishable Self from among these wild reeds of existence and to continue the pursuit all through life, is the challenge the seeker faces.

This metaphor would have been more befitting in earlier chapters where the stress was on the seeker's effort rather than on the nature of the final attainment. Nevertheless, it shows how the way of life of the wise (*jñānins*) differs from that of the ignorant. The wise find themselves immersed in and enjoying the elixir of immortality here and now, while the ignorant, afraid as he is about the multiplicity of existence, the many worlds and his own extinction at death, become immersed in the ocean of sufferings. The freedom to choose either of the paths, one leading to death and the other to Immortality, is ours!

मृत्युप्रोक्तां नचिकेतोऽथ लब्ध्वा
विद्यामेतां योगविधिं च कृत्स्नम् ।
ब्रह्मप्राप्तो विरजोऽभूद् विमृत्यु-
रन्योऽप्येवं यो विदध्यात्ममेव ।। १८ ।।

mṛtyuproktāṁ naciketo'tha labdhvā
vidyām etāṁ yoga-vidhiṁ ca kṛtsnam ।
brahma-prāpto virajo'bhūd vimṛtyur-
anyo'pyevaṁ yo vid adhyātmam eva ।। 18 ।।

Naciketas, then, having gained this wisdom and the entire discipline of yoga (that goes with it), as imparted by Death, attained *Brahman*, and became free from the changefulness of becoming and free from death. So too may anyone else, knowing the self-based Reality, attain *Brahman*.

The envoy of this Upaniṣad, this concluding verse assures the same attainment of Naciketas, to anyone who follows this teaching fully attentive and devout. The mention of the discipline of yoga (*yoga-vidhi*) as though already covered by the Upaniṣad, but in fact not explicit anywhere in the text, may look somewhat out of place. The Yoga System of Patañjali, or the various disciplines recommended therein or in different variant yoga systems, which are far remote from the Vedāntic discipline, are not implied by this reference.

Vedānta in itself, on the other hand, is a science of yoga in a different sense. Yoga means the state of opposite aspects being inseparably united, like the two inseparable yet opposite poles of a magnet. Immutable gold-substance and the mutable ornament form are inseparable in a gold-ornament. So is the inseparability of the changeful aspect of our existence, called *śarīra*, and the unchaning Self-Substance called *ātmā*. Realizing the inseparability of the two, the non-duality of the two, is our final goal. This attainment thus is a state of yoga.

Yet without conceptually differentiating these two aspects, this non-duality would be unattainable. Unless so differentiated, we would continue to take appearances as real. Realizing the Real, therefore, needs, first a conceptual differentiation of opposing factors in us, and then realizing their non-duality. Such a search for Reality also is a yoga discipline, as a means of attainment. Vedānta is thus a science of yoga, both in terms of means and ends.

Even after careful study and meditation of the Upaniṣad, along with all available elucidation and commentary, one may still feel one has not attained what is really to be attained. One may have to go over it again and again with a yogic mind. Vedānta is a *yoga śāstra*, a science of yoga. It needs a yogic mind to get its inner mansion opened up !

शान्तिपाठः

ओम्। सह नाववतु। सह नौ भुनक्तु। सह वीर्यं करवावहै।
तेजस्विनावधीतमस्तु। मा विद्विषावहै ।।
ॐ शान्तिः। शान्तिः। शान्तिः ।।

oṁ: saha nāv avatu । *saha nau bhunaktu* ।
saha vīryaṁ karavāvahai ।
tejasvi nāvadhītam astu । *mā vidviṣāvahai* ।।
oṁ śāntiḥ । *śāntiḥ* । *śāntiḥ* ।।

Glossary

adhyātma jñāna: Loosely translated as spirituality. Strictly, that kind of knowledge which tries to understand the ultimate Reality with one's own existence as the point of reference (from *adhi* to make a basis, and *ātmā* oneself or the self).

ādhyātmika duḥkha: Self-caused sufferings.

ādhibhautika-duḥkha: Sufferings caused by other beings.

ādhidaivika-duḥkha: Sufferings caused by Providence.

adhikārī: One competent for something. In Vedānta, one competent for wisdom.

ajñāna: Ignorance; lack of wisdom. The opposite of *jñāna*.

ajñānin: The ignorant. The opposite of *jñānin*.

akṣara: The imperishable. Refers to the Ultimate Reality, *Brahman*.

amṛta: Immortality or the Immortal Reality. Poetically imagined as the elixir in a golden pot that emerged from the Milk Ocean as a result of churning it by *deva*s and *asura*s together.

amṛtatva: The state of being immortal.

ānanda (*ānandam*): Bliss. To be understood in the context of the Good in Western philosophy as a supreme value. *Sat*, *cit* and *ānanda* are terms conjointly used to describe the Absolute (*Brahman*) in Vedānta. Concerning an individual being, it is to be understood as the value consciousness that enables one to evaluate his own experiences either as pleasant or unpleasant.

aṇu : Atom. Literally, the indivisible.

anuṣṭhāna: Insistent practising of any spiritual discipline.

arati ; The depressive psychological state in which one becomes uninterested in anything in Life.

ātman (*ātmā*): The self (from the root *āt*, to pervade). The invisible reality or substance that pervades all visible forms. Often confused with *jīva*, the soul. Used in slightly altered senses according to the context. The simplest meaning of the word is 'I' or 'oneself'.

avasthātraya: *Avasthā* — states, *traya* — three. The three altering states of consciousness, viz., *jāgarita* (wakefulness), *svapna* (dreaming state) and *suṣupti* (deep sleep).

avyakta : That which is not specific and definable. The opposite of *vyakta*.

avidyā: Nescience or ignorance. That by which one takes the unreal as the Real and the Real as unreal. The root cause of all sufferings.

baḍavāgni: The imaginary fire inherent in ocean. It is because of its presence that ocean never gets overfilled though all the rivers are flowing into it constantly. Poetically conceived that the fire is emitted from the mouth of a mare hidden in the ocean.

bālāḥ : Children; in the wisdom context meaning those of little or no knowledge.

bhavya : That which belongs to the future.

bhūta: That which is of the past.

brahmacarya: The state of being a *brahmācarin*. (See *brahmacārī*).

brahmacārī (*brahmacārin*) : From *Brahman*, the absolute, and *cārin*, one who moves on). One who is moving on the path of *Brahman*. Name of one who is in the first stage of life as a student in a *gurukula*. Such a way of life is called *Brahmacarya*. As a corollary this kind of life would include such disciplines as continence as helpful to realization. But sex is only one of the implied considerations in the discipline of a *brahmacārī*. As evidenced many times in the Upaniṣads, *ṛṣis* have been married and still able to walk the path of *Brahman*.

Brahman: The absolute. Literally, that which is always growing. Also the name of the chief priest in a fire-sacrifice.

brahma-vidyā: The science of *Brahman* or the Absolute. Another name of Vedānta.

cāturvarṇya: The four psychological types or mental colourations as conceived by Indian psychologists. They are brāhmaṇa, kṣatriya, vaiśya, śūdra. Those who are naturally inclined to learning and teaching are brāhmaṇas; those who give leadership to the public with firm mind are kṣatriyas; those who are desirous of becoming wealthy taking to agriculture, rearing cattle, trading and so on are vaiśyas; those who by nature like to live by serving others are śūdras.

cit : Literally, consciousness. The imperishable Reality pervading all the perishable and visible forms is pure consciousness in essence. Hence *Brahman* is designated as *cit*. See *sat* and *ānanda* also.

cetanā : The life principle that animates beings. *Cit* in its functional state.

dakṣiṇā : Free gifts offered to priests and *saṁnyāsins*. It is customary that priests at the conclusion of all Vedic rites, should be pleased by the sacrificer with such gifts.

dama : Checking and turning away of the senses from distractions. One of the prerequisite mental preparations for attaining the wisdom of the Absolute.

dāna : Giving, granting, teaching. A gift given as a religious rite.

dehi (*dehin*): The substance that assumes a visible form or body (*deha*). See *deha*.

deva (*devas*): Gods. Inhabitants of Vedic heaven, meaning the effulgent ones.

devatā : A deity. A god as understood in the context of adoration or worship. Every Vedic hymn has a deity who is praised, a *chandas* or a particular metre in which it is composed, and an *ṛṣi*, the seer who composed it.

deva-yāna : The path of gods. One of the two paths through which the departed souls supposedly go to the other world from where they will not return. Literally, the bright path. Also called *śukla-gati*, the white path. See *pitṛ-yāna*.

dhātā : Another name of Brahma the Creator; literally one who supports.

dhātu : Seven constituent elements of physical body as conceived by the Indian school of medicine. They are: secretions, blood, muscles, fat, bones, marrow, semen.

eṣaṇā-traya : Attachment towards three: wife, children, wealth. All hindrances to liberation.

gārhastya : A householder's life. The second of the four stages in life — *brahmacarya*, *gārhasthya*, *vānaprastha*, *saṁnyāsa*. *Brahmacarya* is the life of a celebate student. *Vānaprastha* is the life after leaving all household responsibilities. *Saṁnyāsa* is a stage in which one renounces everything worldly.

hṛt, *hṛdaya* : Heart.

idam : 'This'. Signifies this world.

iṣṭa-karma : The Vedas enjoin two kinds of pious acts: performing Vedic rites (*iṣṭa karmas*) properly, and the other is *pūrta-karma* (see).

īśvara : The Sanskrit equivalent to God. Literally, one who controls everything.

jagat : The world. Literally, that which is always on the move.

jāgrat : See *avasthātraya*.

jīva : The Sanskrit equivalent to soul. Literally, a being that sustains through breathing. Often confused with *ātmā*, the self.

jijñāsā : The desire to know, inquisitiveness.

jijñāsuḥ : One who is desirous of knowledge.

jñāna : Wisdom. Wisdom concerning the ultimate Reality.

jñānin : One who posses *jñāna*. One who has attained enlightenment. *Jñāna* means Wisdom as contrasted with *karma* (works or ritual). *Jñāna-mārga* or the way of wisdom gives primacy to reason and intuition.

kāraṇa śarīra : The causal body. The body one possesses while in deep sleep.

kārikā : Versified elucidation of a text. A verse of such a work.

karma : Action. All actions are meant by this term, more especially ritualistic actions.

kartā (*kartṛ*) : The doer of *karmas*, the agency of actions.

kartṛtva : The sense of agency of actions.

kratu : Any Vedic fire sacrifice involving killing of animals. Other sacrifices are known as *yajñas*.

kṣara : That which is perishable. All worldly phenomena, including what is known as soul are perishable, and hence constitute *kṣara*.

kṣatra (*kṣatriya*) : The warrior class. One of the four classes of the Indian caste-system. Originally refers to the psychological type which has prowess, brightness, firmness, skill, generosity, dignity and never-absconding as its main characteristics.

loka : The world. That which could be looked at.

madhu: Honey, symbolic of what is valuable in life.

mahat : The great, the adorable.

manana : Intense cogitation on what is directly heard from a Guru (*śravaṇa*), leading finally to full conviction and realization (*nididhyāsana*).

manuṣya : Man; humankind. Literally the descendants of Manu, the thinking being.

martya : Man. Literally , one destined to die.

māyā : Connotes a factor of epistemological and methodological importance in Śaṅkara's Vedānta especially, and in the Upaniṣadic lore generally. Whatever is postulated as the cause of the unreal, spoken of in the most generic of categorical terms in philosophy, as against theology, is to be laid at the door of *māyā*. It is the basis of duality or synergic antinomies. The nearest Western equivalent is the *nagativitat* of Hegel's system.

mokṣa (*mukti*) : Final liberation. Literally, freedom.

muni : A silent recluse.

nididhyāsana : The last stage of gaining wisdom. *Śravaṇa* (hearing the word of instruction from the *guru*) and *manana* (intense cogitation on what is heard from the *guru*) are the two stages preceding.

paṇḍitaḥ : Another word for *jñānin*. One who possesses *paṇḍā*, wisdom.

paṇḍitammanyaḥ : A self-styled *paṇḍitaḥ*.

param : The supreme, the transcendental. An epithet of *Brahman*.

parā-vidyā : Transcendental knowledge. The supreme wisdom represented by the Upaniṣads.

pitr̥s : Manes; the departed souls.

pitr̥-yāna : The path of the manes. One of the two paths through which the departed souls are supposed to travel to the other world from where they would be returning. Also called *kr̥ṣṇa-gati*, the black path. See *deva-yāna*.

pradhāna : Another name for *prakr̥ti*, of the *prakr̥ti-puruṣa* dual concepts of the Sāṁkhya philosophy. Literally, the important.

prakr̥ti : Nature. Literally, that which is always in an active state. This activeness is inherent in the ultimate Reality or *Brahman*. *Brahman* in active state is called *prakr̥ti*.

pramā : Certitude arrived at through valid means or *pramāṇa*.

prāṇa : The vital breath. The functions of vital breath are identified as five, namely, *prāṇa* (going upward), *apāna* (going downward), *vyāna* (that which takes vitality to every part of the body), *samāna* (that which keeps the balance of the body), and *udāna* (that which leaves the body at death).

pravacana: Discourse given by a learned person or a *guru*. After completing formal education under a *guru*, a student has to continue his studies at home through self-study (*svādhyāya*) complemented by attending to discourses of the learned as and when occasion arises. Eventually he too will have to give discourses.

preyas : The common name for the aggregate of worldly values.

pūrta-karma : Any act of pious liberality, such as digging public wells, planting shade trees, building camp sheds for travellers. One of the two kinds of meritorious deeds.

puruṣa : Literally, 'person'. The word is used both in the universal and particular senses. In the universal sense, He is the cosmic person who has the entire cosmos for his body. In this sense He is often called *virāṭ puruṣa*.

rajas : One of the three *guṇas* of *ptakṛti*. The active nature modality represented by red colour.

ṛṣi : A Seer. A wise sage of ancient India who lived generally in the seclusion of forests. They wrote all the hymns of the Vedas as well as the Upaniṣads.They were not necessarily monks and many of them had families.

ṛtam : The eternal reality unfolded as the world order as well as the moral life of man.

sādhana-catuṣṭaya : The common name of the four principal prerequisite qualifications of a seeker. They are *nitya-anitya-vastu-viveka* (discrimination of the eternal and transient values), *vairāgya* (sense of detachment towards transient values), the six disciplines *śama*, *dama*, *uparati, titikṣā*, *śraddhā*, *samādhānam* (see *śama*) and *mumukṣutva*, (desire for liberation)

śakti : Literally prowess. The name of the female counterpart of Śiva, representing the fecundity of nature.

śama : Checking the mind and turning it away from distractions. One of the six qualities to be developed by self-effort as part of spiritual discipline. The other five are *dama* (self-restraint by withdrawing sense-organs from their objects), *uparati* (non-dependence on the external), *titikṣā* (endurance), *śraddhā* (full faith in the words of one's Guru and of the scriptures) and *samādhāna* (having the thought of *Brahman* always in mind).

samādhāna : See *śama*.

saṁnyāsa : To renounce all worldly possessions, attachments and positions.

saṁnyāsin : Renunciate. Monk. One who has given up all worldly possessions and relations.

saṁsāra : Worldly life that passes through a succession of states causing sufferings. Often considered as an ocean. Transmigration of souls is also considered part of it.

sarīra : Literally that which perishes. The physical body or the visible form.

sat-cit-ānanda : Existence, Consciousness. Value experience; the most concise definition of *Brahman* (the Absolute) or *ātman* (the Self).

sat-guru : A true Master.

sat-kāraṇa-vāda : The theory that cause alone is Real and all effects are mere superimpositions projected on to the Real, and therefore all appearances are unreal. This is the theory of Śaṅkara.

sat-kārya-vāda : The theory that effect is as real as cause — Rāmānuja's theory.

sat śiṣya : A true disciple or seeker.

sattva : One of the three nature modalities. It finds expression as purity and is represented by whiteness. Those who are of *sattva* nature will have the inclination to be pure, to know and to teach.

sāyujya : The state of two merged into one. The state in which an individual experiences oneness with the Absolute.

ṣaḍ-bhāva : The six stage of bodily existence. They are: *asti* (existence), *janma* (birth), *vṛddhi* (growth), *pariṇāma* (evolution), *apakṣaya* decline) and *vināśa* (dissolution).

śraddhā : One of the prerequisites on the part of a seeker. Willingness to have full faith in the truthfulness of the word of the Guru and of the scriptures. A necessary stepping stone for *manana* (see *manana*).

śravaṇa : See *manana*.

śreyas : Highest value one can aspire to in life, represented by wisdom, as against *Preyas*.

sthūla-śarīra : The gross body with the help of which consciousness in its wakeful state becomes aware of the gross world.

sukṛta : Literally well done. In the Vedic sense, the meticulous performance of ritual along with the merits achieved through them. Any meritorious deed. The merit achieved through such deeds. One who has done such deeds.

sūkṣma śarīra : The subtle body. The body in which one enjoys subtle objects while dreaming.

suṣupti : See *avasthātraya*.

svādhyāya : Self-study. A student has to continue self-study at home after completing his formal education under a guru and leaving the *gurukula*.

svapna : See *avasthātraya*.

svayambhū : The self-originated. Another name of Brahmā, the Creator.

svayam-dhīraḥ : A self-styled intellectual.

tamas : One of the three modalities of nature, manifesting as inertia and ignorance; represented by darkness.

tapas : Austere self-discipline. Literally, 'heating up'.

tat : That. Stands for the Absolute or *Brahman*, as the Reality to be searched for.

tejas: Brightness, fire.

titikṣā : Endurance of troubles incidental in life, without petulance or self-pity. One of the prerequisite qualities of a seeker.

upaniṣad : When the chapter of *karma* or ritualistic action has been transcended by a religious student or *brahmacārin*, he is ready to receive the posterior philosophical teachings which constitute the Vedānta (i.e., 'the end of the Vedas'). The Vedānta is non-theological; concerned with the Absolute or *Brahman*. The word is said to be derived from *upa*, beside, and *niṣad*, sitting near, so that it is a teaching received by a disciple when he is allowed to sit and listen to philosophical teachings near or by the side of a *guru*.

uparati : The disposition of not being influenced by external matters and considerations in deciding what to do and how to do in the course of life.

vairāgya : Sense of detachment towards everything transient.

Vedas : The earliest of the Indian scriptures, collated into four volumes, named the *Ṛgveda*, *Yajurveda*, *Sāmaveda* and *Adharvavedā*. They praise gods like Indra, Varuṇa, Mitra and other phenomenal gods of nature. They were later overcome by the Upaniṣads. The word *veda* means, knowledge. The Vedas generally stand for ritual (*karma*).

Vedānta : When the Vedic teachings had been revalued in philosophical terms by later *ṛṣis* (sages), a body of literature called Vedānta arose in the history of Indian thought. These often go contrary to the Vedic tendencies of ritual and obligations, announcing freedom and stressing Self-realization. Later we find Śaṅkara, Rāmānuja and Madhva, referred to as three typical Vedāntic philosophers, although the Gurus of the Vedāntic line (*paramparā*) are many. (See also *Upaniṣad*).

vibhu : The all-pervading.

vidyā : Knowledge. That by which one understands the Real as the real and the unreal as the unreal .

vijñāna : Any specific or applied form of knowledge or wisdom.

Viṣṇu : The second of the Hindu trinity, of which Brahmā, the creator is the first, and Maheśvara or Śiva, the last. Śiva is also the destroyer. Viṣṇu is referred to as the preserver, although taken by themselves each of them is in turn preserver and destroyer. This results from the fusing of three cosmological and psychological currents of religious thought in India.

viveka : Discrimation. The natural capability in one to discriminate the eternal and transient values in life.

Yati : One of self-restraint.

yoga : (from the root *yuj*, to join). Psychic union of the self with the Self, just as an ornament finds its oneness with gold. As contemplative method of expression, the way of expressing an inexpressible reality by showing its two opposite sides and leaving the unitive meaning to be grasped by the reader or seeker. For example, attaining immortality and crossing over death are two expressions meaning the same. But these two expressions are opposite in nature. They have in between them a meaning that cannot be expressed as it is. Equivalent to the Platonic method of 'Dialectics' of the West.

yoga-śāstra : The science of yoga. As a method of scientific thinking, equivalent to dialectics as conceived by Plato. The *Bhagavad Gītā* claims itself to be a *yoga-śāstra*.

Index